# Hacking Work

'Bill and Josh will help you break free of the shackles of how business is traditionally done and leverage the power of hacking to solve your company's most intractable problems'

Eric Ryan, chief brand architect and co-founder, Method

'The way we're working today sucks. If you've realized that fact, and your organization isn't doing anything about it, *Hacking Work* will help you achieve your results and not go insane waiting for those around you to wake up'

Cali Ressler and Jody Thompson, co-creators of the
Results-Only Work Environment (ROWE) and co-authors of
*Why Work Sucks and How to Fix It*

'Anyone frustrated by burdensome rituals and processes can now take responsibility for their own success. Jensen and Klein irreverently and cleverly show us the power of hacking work and taking responsibility for one's own success. The ideas within *Hacking Work* will foster the innovation and creativity so badly needed in these times'

Dave Ulrich, professor, Ross School of Business,
and co-author of *The Why of Work*

'*Hacking Work* is a refreshing antidote to what passes for business wisdom today. Sure, organizations need structure and processes. But to get your work done, you need this book. It's the perfect manual for long-overdue corporate insurgency. Find a way to hide it on your expense account!'

Thomas H. Davenport, President's Distinguished Professor
of IT and Management, Babson College,
and co-author of *Analytics at Work*

'The time has come to accept that our outdated business precepts are unraveling. Jensen and Klein reveal a new hope: businesses succeeding and innovating in spite of themselves. A brave new world is upon us – we can embrace it and excel or deny it and die'

Jim McCarthy, consultant and former EVP,
Strategic Development, CITGO Petroleum

'*Hacking Work* is a badly needed wake-up call urging executives to remove the manifold limitations standing in the way of true innovation. This book could not be more timely: As our economies move out of recession, it is high time to question and redesign every aspect of doing business that creates obstacles to competitiveness'

Jean-Daniel Gerber, State Secretary,
Ministry of the Economy, Switzerland

## ABOUT THE AUTHORS

Bill Jensen is CEO of the Jensen Group, a change consulting firm he founded in 1985, and an internationally acclaimed speaker. He lives in Morristown, New Jersey.

Josh Klein hacks institutions, computer networks, hardware and more. He consults for groups such as Microsoft, Nokia and the U.S. intelligence community. He lives in New York.

# HACKING WORK

**BREAKING**

**STUPID RULES**

**FOR SMART RESULTS**

Bill Jensen and Josh Klein

PORTFOLIO
PENGUIN

PORTFOLIO PENGUIN

Published by the Penguin Group
Penguin Books Ltd, 80 Strand, London WC2R 0RL, England
Penguin Group (USA) Inc., 375 Hudson Street, New York, New York 10014, USA
Penguin Group (Canada), 90 Eglinton Avenue East, Suite 700, Toronto, Ontario, Canada M4P 2Y3
(a division of Pearson Penguin Canada Inc.)
Penguin Ireland, 25 St Stephen's Green, Dublin 2, Ireland (a division of Penguin Books Ltd)
Penguin Group (Australia), 250 Camberwell Road, Camberwell, Victoria 3124, Australia
(a division of Pearson Australia Group Pty Ltd)
Penguin Books India Pvt Ltd, 11 Community Centre, Panchsheel Park, New Delhi – 110 017, India
Penguin Group (NZ), 67 Apollo Drive, Rosedale, North Shore 0632, New Zealand
(a division of Pearson New Zealand Ltd)
Penguin Books (South Africa) (Pty) Ltd, 24 Sturdee Avenue, Rosebank, Johannesburg 2196, South Africa

Penguin Books Ltd, Registered Offices: 80 Strand, London WC2R 0RL, England

www.penguin.com

First published in the United States of America by
Portfolio Penguin, a member of Penguin Group (USA) Inc. 2010
First published in Great Britain by Portfolio Penguin 2010

1

Printed in Great Britain by Clays Ltd, St Ives plc

A CIP catalogue record for this book is available from the British Library

ISBN: 978–0–670–91950–5

www.greenpenguin.co.uk

Penguin Books is committed to a sustainable future
for our business, our readers and our planet.
The book in your hands is made from paper
certified by the Forest Stewardship Council.

# Dedication

To the underground army of benevolent hackers
who are saving business from itself,
one bad act at a time.
—Bill and Josh


To my folks, for giving me the courage to love what I do and to do
what I love. They taught me to hack the right way—with courage
and respect—and I thank them for it.
— Josh

# Contents

# HACKING
# WORK

# PREFACE

# PSSSSSST...

**For several years** we have foraged in the back alleys of business, arranging clandestine meetings with the bad boys and girls of work. Empty cans of Red Bull, pizza crusts, and shredded nondisclosure agreements littered our meeting places.

"Psssssst. How do you *really* get everything done? What are your work-arounds? The ones that keep your company afloat, keep customers happy, teammates employed, and keep you doing your best? We want the world to know about the power of benevolent hacking."

Who are we, and why do that? We're just two guys who have dedicated our professional lives to finding work-arounds to corporate bullshit.

Bill's day job is making it easier to get stuff done. Over the course of two decades, he has asked over five hundred thousand people around the world what makes their work so hard and complicated. C-suite dwellers love his findings on simplicity. Bill advises executives and their troops on how to work smarter by making work simpler. He has consulted with many of the biggest companies in the world, local and federal governments, even the U.S. Navy SEALs.

But Bill's most important advice has always hit a brick wall. His research has consistently found that the number one source of work complexity is built into every company's infrastructure—the tools and processes we are supposed to use to get our work done. They are designed to help the *company* succeed but are not built for the success of the *individuals* who do the work.

Business's failure to deal with this obvious problem is one of its biggest problems. Yet the reaction from most graybeards has been decidedly chilly: "Let's not go there."

"Arrrrgh! How do I get these people to listen?" Bill wondered. Addressing this problem would be game changing . . . a true competitive advantage for every company and the end of so much frustration and wasted effort for every individual.

The answer finally appeared over drinks at a TED (Technology, Entertainment, Design) conference. "Change the approach," said Josh, who had just presented how he had hacked the work ethic of crows by training the birds to bring him money. "If their executives won't listen, let's show employees how to hack around their problems."

From his early days of snarfing Wi-Fi passwords in Seattle to his recent consulting work with U.S. intelligence agencies, Josh has been hacking technologies and putting them back together to great effect. Some years ago, he noticed that this kind of systems thinking could be applied to people and organizations, not just to technology.

As he helped companies all over the world make the most of their technologies, Josh saw firsthand how unwilling people are to question what they take for granted—and how powerful it can be to do so. From megacorporations to start-ups, from investors to students, he found that while everyone talked about innovation, few were willing to pull the trigger that would kill an old business model or to embrace the changes that would create a new one.

Josh's constant questioning of the status quo helped him publish a novel by giving it away for free, got him invited to speak at the most hard-to-access conference in the world by telling them what they were doing wrong, and enabled him to double his salary by quitting his job.

Between Josh's tech savvy and Bill's business background, our back-alley conversations produced straight talk from thousands of people. From those on the front lines serving customers to the geeks in corporate server closets, the workforce told us what they're not telling their bosses.

This book is a tough love letter: There's an underground army of benevolent hackers out there who are saving business from itself, one bad act at a time. This is their story.

Ours: Two guys hacking the future, one day at a time. Finding better ways to get stuff done and having fun along the way.

BILL@HACKINGWORK.COM

JOSH@HACKINGWORK.COM

# WOOT!

We are exposing the cheat codes for work and sharing them with the world.

Once employees know how to hack their work, everything's up for grabs—how we work, when and where we work, how we define effectiveness and success . . .

Everything.

Benevolent hackers see the future and pull us toward it, in whatever ways work best.

**W00t!** Expression of joy and excitement '80s hackers used to disguise that they had gained root access—(the most fundamental level of control)—to someone's system. Root was replaced with w00t!

# 1

# SAVING BUSINESS FROM ITSELF, ONE BAD ACT AT A TIME

> If you think you are too small to be effective, you
> have never been in bed with a mosquito.
>
> —Betty Reese, American pilot

**Business is broken.** We all know it, even if we're scared to admit it.

Most of us feel screwed, and many of us feel helpless to change it. We have become slaves to our infrastructure—to business's controlling tools, procedures, and mandates. Something's got to give. Something already has.

Richard Saunders is living proof. He works for one of the top banks in the world. One of those institutions that did its job so well in 2008 that it helped dig us into the worst financial hole we've been in since the Great Depression. Yeah, one of those firms.

Richard's job is to provide the bank's clients—law firms and courts holding over $50 million in escrow for their clients—the reports they need to keep track of all those assets. His team takes thousands of different statements and consolidates them all into simple, easy-to-read reports for clients. It's like drinking from a fire hose so others don't have to.

Then there's his work for the senior team. As the crisis unfolded, they wanted their own custom-made distillations—lots of them. The problem was that nothing in this growing data stream helped serve clients better, increased the value of service provided, or predicted catastrophes. They were just more detailed rearview mirrors the executives used to calm themselves with the illusion of greater control. Even worse: What the execs *really* wanted—useful, insightful analysis—couldn't be easily produced using the software provided by corporate IT.

Poor Richard. What to do? Work twenty-nine hours a day, ten days a week, to manually create these reports and the much-needed analysis? Get stressed out, skip family time—all to soothe the shattered nerves of his senior execs? No way. He hacked the system.

Knowing that the software was written in the programming language Visual Basic and connected to a simple database, he used Microsoft Access to link to the database's back end. Getting the database password was easy enough. "I just called the software vendor," Richard says, "softened him up, and he readily gave it to me. Once I had that, I was able to tap into the database and pull all the data I needed—and make massive changes on the fly."

Would the bank's auditors and IT security guys freak out if they knew that Richard had hacked their system and had almost full access to all customer data? You bet. But since his hack, Richard has become incredibly productive and is the companywide authority on these types of accounts. He's now the go-to hero with all those senior execs because he's been able to give them a lot more than just data dumps—and he's preempted a ton of problems for clients along the way.

If they only knew the full story. Says Richard (not his real name, of course), "As a result of this hack, I keep senior management off our backs, so we're able to keep doing more for our clients with less."

He's not alone in believing that he has to change the rules for getting things done if he's going to increase his productivity and achieve better results for the firm. Many in our workforce are coming to the same conclusion.

Evers Pearce, a university employee in Oxford who had his budget slashed to nothing, is another example. Instead of accepting this edict, he funded his projects with £37,000 by selling on eBay what he was supposed to be throwing away—furniture, engine parts, construction waste—and wrangled the income back into the finance system.

Elizabeth is a manager whose bosses would not approve her customer satisfaction project—even though the entire senior team deemed it crucial—because the payoff wouldn't be realized for at least four financial quarters. So she secretly videotaped customers voicing their complaints as well as their wish lists for enhancing the company's product lines and posted it on YouTube. Within days, there was enough public outcry that senior management reversed their decision and approved her project.

One new hire, Matt, so disagreed with his employer's assessment process that he Googled "performance assessment" and created a seventeen-question mash-up that matched *his* career goals—not just the company's goals for him. His manager and the HR department were shocked and pissed off, but he had spent months refining his performance tool. He'd done his homework, seeking advice from one of the gurus in the assessment field whom he'd contacted through LinkedIn. With the support of his co-workers, Matt stood his ground, and management ended up using his assessment in conjunction with their own.

What's even more telling about this challenge to the status quo is that it came in the midst of an economic crisis and a horrible job market. "My career path and my future can't be just about keeping *this* job," says Matt. "It's the mix of projects I work on, and how I improve my own performance at each successive job. I'm better at what I do—for my company and customers as well as for me—because I hacked their assessment process and helped create one that worked for *me*."

These are not isolated incidents.

Change is coming, and it's coming in every workplace, in every industry, from every generation across the globe.

We're outing the biggest open secret of the working world: Today's top performers are taking matters into their own hands. They are bypassing sacred structures and breaking all sorts of rules just to get their work done.

We're exposing the cheat codes for work and sharing them with the world.

Every day in every workplace, benevolent rule breakers like these are ensuring that business succeeds despite itself. They are reinventing how to approach productivity and how to consistently achieve *morebetterfaster* results.

They're hacking work, and you can, too.

Business's love of lingering bureaucracy, legacy technologies, and deeply embedded procedures is killing us. More and more of us are finding that our work tools and structures are completely out of sync with what we need to do our best. Most of our daily needs, dreams, desires, and goals are far ahead of our employers' technological, procedural, and social adoption curves.

The bad guys in this story are not economic turmoil or traumatic market shifts; nor are they your boss or even your company. The bad guys are the tools, processes, procedures, and structures we all use to get work done.

Business's infrastructure is not keeping up with us. That which was supposed to help us now dictates too much of what we *can't* get done. Our tools have become more bossy than our bosses.

What makes this story so urgent and timely isn't just what a pain in the ass all this is, or even that it's costing us our jobs—it's that it's so devastating at the same time there are quantum leaps everywhere *but* work. Even though business spent $1.5 trillion on info tech in 2010,[1] the tools we have outside of work are leapfrogging past what we use on the job.

When a twelve-year-old can gather information faster, process it better, reference more diverse professionals, and get volunteer guidance from better sources than you can at work, how can you pretend you're competitive? When you have more empowering tools in your mobile phone for your personal use than what your company provides or approves for your projects—how can you work within, or be saved from, devastating market forces?

You can't.

So what *can* you do? Start hacking.

Start taking the usual ways of doing things and work around them to produce improved results. Bend the rules for the good of all. That's what benevolent hackers do.

What was once shunned as bad is now the new good, because it challenges outdated tools and procedures that refuse to budge. We've uncovered what nobody wanted you to know: You no longer have to play the game the way your company insists you do. The illusion of corporate control is being shattered in the name of personal efficiency.

Once employees know how to hack their work, everything's up for grabs—how we work, when and where we work, how we define effectiveness and success . . . everything.

Want to work smarter, not harder? Start hacking.

Want to be a better manager, leader, or entrepreneur? Embrace the hackers around you and learn from them.

Want to leave a legacy and make a real difference? Start hacking.

Benevolent hackers are on a mission: to save business from itself, and you from business.

Come join our thriving underground army of heroes. You will hack work-arounds big and small, high-tech and no-tech, risky and safe, enduring and ephemeral. You will improve the productivity of your company, yourself, and everyone you touch.

# 2

# YOU WERE BORN TO HACK

Dare to be naïve.

—R. Buckminster Fuller, architect and futurist

## THERE IS NO THEM, ONLY US

Have you ever called the person in charge of a process and negotiated an exception to a deadline or a rule? How about emailing a company file to yourself at a personal address just so you could work on it at home? Have you ever bent the rules just to check off more to-dos? If the answer is yes, would you say you were more efficient and effective because of it?

Then you're a hacker.

You were born to hack. All children are.

That's because hacking is the act of understanding a system well enough to take it apart, play with its inner workings, and do something better with it. This desire to disassemble and improve is natural and built into all of us. Most children are fascinated with figuring out how innovation and creation work, and it all begins by taking things apart.

## HACKING WORK DEFINED

**Hacking work is forbidden innovation.** It is the act of getting what you need to do your best by exploiting loopholes and creating work-arounds. It is taking the usual ways of doing things and bypassing them to produce improved results.

Hacking work is getting the system to work for you, not just the other way around . . . making it easier to do great work.

Benevolent hackers see the future and pull us toward it. Every day in every workplace, hackers are the heroes who ensure that business succeeds *despite* itself. Their innovations plug the holes in business's strategies, structures, tools, and processes with work-arounds. Their efforts change bureaucracies into meritocracies—with or without permission.

Bill began by disassembling his favorite toy, Mr. Machine, and too many of Mom's appliances to name. Later, he figured out how to hack systems of authority, like using the principal's office and budget to organize and fund Senior Cut Day in high school. Josh figured out the authority thing a little earlier. At age seven, he hacked the tooth fairy. His hacker's note explained that because of inflation, the price of teeth had just risen from a quarter to a dollar. His parents still have the tooth and note, documenting how he reworked the fairy's decision-making process.

Think back. Surely you have similar stories. It may have been reinventing your mom's favorite recipe, reprogramming the family's electronics, or redesigning the routines behind your allowance to yield the highest reward for the least effort. This is what children do. They hack to learn, to grow, to imagine completely new possibilities. It's a natural approach, and it works. Taking something apart and reconstructing the pieces has long been shown to be one of the most effective ways to master any subject.

Unfortunately, most of us grew up. That is, we came to accept that hacking things was the wrong way to learn. The right way is to sit in neat little rows, keep quiet until called upon, raise our hand to speak, and always, always follow a planned, predictable process laid out by an authority figure.

Hacking, bad. Tsk, tsk. Learning by following the rules and paying attention to the boss at the head of the class, good. Gold star!

## GREAT HACKERS NEVER GROW UP

The best hackers among us never stayed within the lines of their coloring books. They never allowed childlike wonder to be squeezed out of them. From kindergarten through university and now in the workplace, these hackers can't figure out why anyone would give up digging their fingers into everything just to learn how things work and how they could be changed. That's core to any hacker's drive: unleashing the untapped potential in everything; reworking the status quo so it works better.

In our workplace, that means removing barriers that slow us down and frustrate us, giving us more power to do what needs to be done. Benevolent hackers are the personification of all that is good in our workforce. Against all odds, they *will* find a way to do their best.

Among the most successful hackers, the alpha geeks, this is a natural proclivity that just can't be denied. They are a passionate lot, and what they do at work and play is just a side effect of that passion.

That's how Josh was once given a brand-new Mac by a friend.

"What's wrong with it?" he asked.

"Nothing," was the matter-of-fact reply.

And that was the problem. The operating system was reliable

enough that there was nothing to fix, and the hardware was sturdy and well constructed, so there was no need to take it apart. Where's the fun in that? To an alpha, that's a dead end. To this day, Josh's friend still runs Windows. Lots to fix there!

Whether you're an alpha geek, an occasional dabbler, or a corporate minion who desperately needs to get out of bureaucratic purgatory, the motivation to hack always falls within the same categories:

> **Curiosity:** "I wonder what would happen if . . ."
> **Imagination:** "Gee, wouldn't it be cool if . . . ?"
> **Drive:** "I will not accept 'no.' There has got to be a better way!"

This is what makes hacking work so powerful and necessary. Our bosses are too busy trying to figure out how to get their companies out of death spirals to rethink their work designs. Enter you: full of childlike wonder and enthusiasm, and—most important—with the on-the-ground experience needed to solve problems that are plaguing us all. You're just the kind of hero business needs, especially if it's too stuck in its ways to know it.

That's an important principle to remember as you think about hacking work. Hacking doesn't have to begin with a solution in mind. You don't necessarily have to have the right answer, nor does business necessarily have the wrong one. Hacking begins with "What if . . . ?" and "I wonder why . . ."

Hacking works because it's not really about your boss or bureaucracy or that stupid procedure. It's you standing on a chair with a blanket for a cape, leaping off with the confidence that you're about to fly into the world of unlimited possibilities!

## EVERYBODY EVERYWHERE HACKS

Let's begin our relationship with complete honesty: You are no virgin when it comes to this stuff. You've been hacking for years.

And you're not the only one who hacks. So does he, she, us, them, the young and the old, the über-elite and the clueless, the slackers and the fast trackers. . . . Everybody everywhere hacks.

New technologies have so radically changed the social, cultural, and economic landscape of human connections that, increasingly,

## WHY HACK: WIIFM?

**W**hat's in it for me if I hack or if I embrace the hackers within my firm?

**Individuals Win:**
- Easier to do great work
- Greater control over your own destiny
- Truly working smarter, not harder . . . tailoring a lot more to your individual needs
- Better qualified in your own job. . . less dependence on your company's survival
- Better sex, longer life, more meaningful relationships
- More fun

**The Company Wins:**
- Easier for every individual to do great work: which translates into . . .
- Unleashes everyone's capacity, creativity, innovations: which translates into . . .
- *Morebetterfastercheaper:* which translates into . . .
- Creates new and sustainable competitive advantages
- Reinvents your relationship with your workforce: much more symbiotic win/win
- Did we mention *morebetterfastercheaper*?

everyone participates as hackers: Are you looking for a picture of a mermaid on roller skates to use in a presentation? Use Flickr! Want the best deal on a new product? Use RetailMeNot, BuyWithMe, Ebates, or Stingier! Want to run for president of the United States without owing your soul to special-interest groups? Bypass how it's usually done and go directly to the masses for millions of $25 donations! Want to max out your 64 GB iPod Touch? Find what you need on ThePirateBay or Spotify or use your (or your kid's) university's free file-sharing system!

It's finally OK to admit it. Whether it's how you used a social connection or how you scored those tickets or that latest discount or freebie: You are a hacker. There are no non-hackers, only those who prefer to be perceived that way.

The global economy is moving so fast that most of its established systems can't keep up. That, combined with new technologies, creates opportunities to be exploited by everyone everywhere: Hacking any system that is too slow, too bureaucratic, too unresponsive, or too costly is now part of the global economic engine.

It began with hard-core geeks who wanted to learn whatever could be learned. Their guiding principle: Information wants to be free.

All knowledge is good. The only rule was, "Don't be a dick." If that meant sharing a codec so that any DVD can be watched anywhere or sharing backdoors into a car's computer system to improve its suspension—so be it. And if the masses benefit by making this information easily available . . . well, that's just being a good global citizen, right?

Now this practice has been mainstreamed. It's no longer just geeks who hack corporate systems. It's the founder of a three-person business in a small town you've never heard of halfway around the world, who believes she can take market share from the industry leader. She Googles "Google hacks" and instantly gets an extensive list of one-line queries she can use to study her competitors' client contacts, patent filings, contract documents, purchase orders, and more.

If mission-critical information like this is as easy to find as asking

Google, why should businesses be surprised that you—one of their star performers—would be cocky and brazen enough to hack your own workplace?

They shouldn't be. As a matter of fact, they put hacking in play and set the example for you years ago.

Employers have been hacking *your* systems since birth—every time they wanted to sell you something. Viral marketing was used to influence your mom to buy a specific diaper or detergent. Later, those same companies used your social network and the data they collected about you online to make you believe that their jeans or beer or mobile phone or sneakers were so cool that you just *had* to buy them. Then they created phone trees that use lots of your time instead of their customer service rep's, because that's more cost-effective for them. Even debt collectors are tapping into your Facebook page to monitor any purchases and finances you discuss with friends.

The list is endless—you have been hacked by somebody's employer your whole life! All in the name of their bottom line and market share.

It's time to hack back. After all, if it's good for them, it's good for you—turnabout is fair play.

SIDETRIP

## A SHORT HISTORY OF HACKING'S JOURNEY FROM GOOD TO BAD TO GOOD

**Hacking began** as a very good thing. It borrowed its name from **1960s** MIT students—members of a model train group who modified trains, tracks, and switches to make them perform better. They later hacked MIT's mainframe computer to improve its performance, which is how the term *hacking* became associated with techies and their exploits.

*(continued)*

**1970s:** Phone "phreakers" discovered that a cheap whistle produced a 2,600 Hz sound that allowed free calls over AT&T's long-distance switching systems. Among the perpetrators who built "blue boxes" for free calls: college kids Steve Wozniak and Steve Jobs, future founders of Apple Computer.

**1980s:** The 1983 movie *WarGames* showed that anyone could break into any computer. Hackers become mainstream bad guys. Many gleaned an additional message from the film: Hacking gets you girls. Hacking takes off. In 1986, West German and KGB operatives try to break into U.S. government systems through University of California computers. And between 1988 and 1995, there was a major crackdown on the explosion of malicious hacks.

**1990s:** Hacks and hacking tools explode as the Internet makes everything available to everybody. Malicious hacks—"spoofing," "phishing," and worse—continue through the present day, but there's also a resurgence of good hacks. Many renew hacking's original mission: to improve overall performance.

**2000s:** By the end of the decade, hacking has both regained its luster as a good thing (White Hat Hackers) and attracted more bad people (Black Hatters—from script kiddies to the Russian mafia). There are also Gray Hatters, who expose vulnerabilities in systems in order to improve them, with no malicious intent. This book is an example of a Gray Hat hack.

**3**

# WHAT'S NEW, WHAT'S NOT, WHAT'S THE MOST COMMON HACK?

Discovery consists of seeing what everybody has
seen and thinking what nobody has thought.

—Heraclitus, Greek philosopher

## HACKING WORK IS NOT NEW

Hacking work has been a hallmark of success since the very first bureaucracy—from Archimedes to Galileo to the Founding Fathers, breaking and reinventing the rules is the foundation for innovation.

Agriculture was most likely a work hack: Instead of always roaming over the next hill every time the clan needed grain, someone cleverly figured out that they could grow it closer to camp. Gronk, their leader, neither asked for nor approved this change. And his head of manufacturing—Club and Spear Guy—most certainly felt threatened. The clan's operations would have to change to meet the needs of its new farmers. Still, some hacker found a more efficient way to feed everyone and human history was forever changed.

Commerce, arts, sports, education, war, agriculture, medicine, and government have all been pushed forward by hackers. Thousands of years after Gronk, farmers were having a tough time plowing their soil, so John Deere hacked a work-around by forging the first steel plow out of a saw blade. During World War I, French, German, and American ace fighter pilots stormed into factories and hacked the production of planes, working backward from the needs of the pilot. Their hacks pushed the aviation industry out of its infancy. The history of hacking *is* the history of innovation.

The art of hacking has now crept into most every aspect of society.

There are life hacks, for those who want work-arounds for living a simpler life. There are instruction manual hacks—if it weren't for the *Harry Potter* series, the *Dummies* books would rank among the world's best sellers.

Do-it-yourselfers are reworking nearly every product to meet their own needs. For example, "I look at Ikea more as a hardware store or as a component store than as a place that sells items," says Randall Kramer, a Chicago-based furniture designer. "I see many of the things they sell as a building block. It's not that they've dropped the ball—it's like they left it for you to individualize or customize it."[1] Even the lowly calculator has a dedicated base of hackers who build their own versions of Whac-A-Mole, Tetris, or new operating systems into their devices. "It's all about taking a limited device and doing the impossible with it," says hobbyist Brandon Wilson.[2]

## WHAT IS NEW:
## THE OPENNESS AND AUDACITY TO EMBRACE
## SMALL BAD ACTS AS THE NEW GOOD

Originally, we thought this book would be about Gen Y, the Millennials. We know that this generation of hackers already has back-of-the-hand knowledge with many tools to do things their parents and managers never tried or imagined, and as soon as they hit critical mass in the workforce—*wham* . . . watch out!

We still see them as a force to be reckoned with (see chapter 8), but the deeper we dug, the more obvious it became that hacking work is not just a Young Turk thing. It's a massive, ongoing, leaderless underground response to feeling screwed.

We met with every generation currently working, in almost every industry, and found a pervasive and universal problem: The design of work isn't meeting the needs of the people who do the work. And nobody's happy about that!

What's changing—and why now is the time to release your inner hacker—is a growing openness about challenging the tools and procedures we're handed. Boomers and X'ers are seeing Millennials hack what's broken and then share what they changed with their friends. That open sharing of hacks among teammates wasn't happening until very recently.

As Microsoft founder Bill Gates said at a recent TED conference: "There are some very important problems that don't get worked on naturally. . . . The market does not drive the scientists, the communicators, the thinkers, the governments, to do the right things. And only by paying attention to these things, and having brilliant people who care and draw other people in, can we make as much progress as we need to."

The new openness around hacking work makes it possible to draw in brilliant people like you to fix what market forces aren't fixing.

The market doesn't care that corporate IT is more of a barrier to you than an enabler. (That includes many of Gates's own products.) The market doesn't care that HR is still living in the 1950s, shoving one-way assessment tools down your throat. The market doesn't care that your manager sucks or that she's in your way or that she can't build a team. The market simply doesn't work on problems at your level.

And that's why hacking is so powerful. That's why it works. That's why it's coming out of the closet now. Hacking fixes many of business's chronic problems that wouldn't have been fixed otherwise.

That idea is spreading. A recent conference on educational reform was titled "Hacking Education," and a session at the 2010 Davos World Economic Forum was titled "Hacking Management." Hacking as a positive force for change has come of age.

## TODAY'S MOST COMMON HACK

Need more of a nudge to draw outside the lines and start breaking some rules? Just consider how many corporate rules were made to be broken because they needlessly make your life harder. For example, Andy's company uses Microsoft's SharePoint servers, and his bosses insist that all presentations be delivered in PowerPoint. Trouble was, when Andy needed to collaborate with others on PowerPoint slides, it took forever to upload to SharePoint and then another chunk of forever to download from it. Every presentation began with the same collective groan: "Pain in the ass!"

While home from college one weekend, Andy's son showed him how to use Google Documents. What a difference! Now Andy's teammates do all their work collaboratively, from work or home or while on the road—easily, quickly—and save it to PowerPoint only at the last minute, just in time to upload to the SharePoint server. "We do this all the time to make presentations to bosses whose brains would explode if you don't use PowerPoint," says Andy. "No one's ever the wiser."

Once they got comfortable bypassing corporate IT, his team went even further. They now use Google's social media, Buzz, for most of their team updates and on-the-fly meetings.

Andy's story tracks perfectly with one of the most common hacks we found: jumping IT's firewall and working around their restrictions and tools in open computing environments, then bringing the work back over the firewall and presenting it to bosses as if the corporate tools had actually been used.

All this is necessary because the tools that so many of us are given to use are corporate centered—designed to help the company succeed, but not necessarily designed for our needs. However, the universe of tools available to us in the outside world, like Gmail and Google Docs and iPhone apps, are user centered—easily customized for each individual's needs. (We'll dive into this problem in a lot more detail in chapter 7.)

## THREE KEY TAKEAWAYS

1. **Hacking work is not new.**
2. **What is new** is the audacity to openly embrace hacking as an **amazing innovation engine** to solve business's most chronic problems. But no matter how benevolent the end result, what makes a hacker a hacker is bypassing, reworking, and bending the rules that keep you from doing your best. Standard operating procedures be damned.
3. **Hacking work is not just for techies:** You don't need to be a techno-geek to do a great hack. While many hacks do require technological work-arounds, some of the best solutions involve simple changes in relationships and sharing information differently, using tools you already have.

## SMALL, LOW-TECH WORK-AROUNDS: BIG RESULTS

Lots of valuable hacks involve only tiny changes. They can be low-tech and low-risk and still create big results. Sean's story is a perfect example. His hacks are neither extraordinary nor revolutionary and mostly involved changes in relationships. But his work-arounds saved his sanity, his soul, and many jobs.

Sean works for a major telecom company, creating computer training for their billing systems, project management, and knowledge-sharing tools. Eight years ago, his team knew they would function best within HR, but the gods of corporate structures knew better, so they got stuck reporting to the CIO.

During an org chart shuffle, a new CIO showed up with plans to reduce spending. Danger, danger: Layoff alert! If Sean had been a typical midmanager, many of his team members would have been on their way out the door. Fortunately for them, Sean is a hacker.

He convinced the CIO that a great way to reduce his budget would be to off-load Sean's team onto HR, and he then dangled a carrot in front of the head of HR. With his team reporting to her, she could increase her ability to impact the company's bottom line.

**Hacking Round 1:** Two relationship work-arounds, resulting in multiple jobs saved.

A while later, Sean's team was told to stop working on one of their ongoing projects—it was in direct conflict with what the CIO had hired an outside consulting firm to do. Sean asked if they could finish a simple prototype at zero cost and use it to gather feedback to be passed on to the consultants. A year later, the CIO's officially sanctioned project was canceled, having produced not a single result, and Sean's "prototype" was already widely adopted throughout the company. Six years after that, Sean's team's work is still in use.

**Hacking Round 2:** A process work-around. Prototyping the program was just a ruse. Sean knew that once users had access to his team's program, it would take off. Just as in the outside marketplace, where people are clamoring for solutions *now*, a hacker's ability to gain rapid adoption of his ideas can outmuscle and outlast lesser solutions from corporate.

Then came the economic meltdown. All of Sean's spending was suspended until further notice. In his own words: "With a large team, a pile of commitments to internal customers, and no money for anything but salaries, I kept thinking: What are we going to do now? After lots of agonizing, it hit me. A better question is: What are we *not* going to do? For the first time in years, I'm free to say no to the mind-numbing, soul-sucking projects that we foolishly agreed to do when we thought saying yes to everything was the best way to survive. My team is now focusing on the projects most likely to succeed and delivering real value for the organization. The bad economy has actually set up our next adventure!"

Sean didn't commit heresy. He didn't set out to free the proletariat or consciously break the rules or piss people off. He just couldn't accept the status quo and had to find work-arounds. That's all that hacking is: getting what you need to do your best by creating work-arounds that produce better results.

But, boy, did he succeed! During the past eight years, he saved his teammates' jobs as well as his own, and together they saved a business from itself by outperforming a CIO and his high-priced consultants. That last result cannot be overstated. Even if his boss won't happily admit it, in this one case Sean served the entire company better than the CIO did. Great hacking is not about saving yourself at the expense of the company. It's about saving yourself *and* the company!

Finally, faced with dire financial restraints, Sean donned a blanket for a cape, stood on a chair, and leapt off into a world where it's possible to say no to a lot more stupid work!

Extraordinary results from ordinary work-arounds. That's the power that's in your hands right now.

## WORKING AROUND POWER STRUCTURES

Hacking work is happening in all kinds of workplaces. LeeAnne Del Rio is a teacher trying to change the educational system. In her own words: "There are lots of us out there supporting the efforts of LISTA [Leaders Imagining Solutions Through Action] to wean students off the quiz-for-the-right-answer approach and teach them to trust their brilliance to figure out a lot more on their own. Our goal

# WORK-AROUNDS FROM THE FIELD

**Changing the Rules** from Raveena, a corporate trainer who confides to her trainees that because of budget constraints, much of what she provides "sucks." So she sends her trainees to free online sources outside of the company. Then, after testing them on what they learned, she validates their certificates in required courses they never attended. Result: They consistently learn more this way.

**Jumping the Firewall** from a team at one of the world's largest credit card companies that secretly hosts some of its information on outside servers. (Don't worry, there's no secure customer data outside the firewall—only internal information the team members need to do their jobs.) Nobody listened to their complaints that IT's restrictions hurt their ability to meet their deadlines and accountabilities. So several years ago, they hacked a work-around. Since then, their senior execs hold them up as examples of what can be done with decreased

is big changes. But in the meantime, I have to keep my job and pay my bills."

As a part-time sociology instructor at a community college, Lee-Anne often found that she was left out of the departmental loop. Even though part-timers make up 75% of the teachers at most colleges in California, they don't get invited to faculty meetings, take part in board meetings, or become involved in departmental decision making. Denied the opportunity to make a real difference within the system, LeeAnne took matters into her own hands.

"With no authority or permission to do so, I started a Web page and online community for sociology and psychology instructors to share resources and syllabi, communicate ideas, and chat. Everyone resources and budgets. If they only knew what had to be done to deliver those results.

**Expense Report Makeover** from Danny, who was tired of carrying pockets full of receipts while traveling for business. What made it worse was the six to eight hours a month he had to spend doing his expense reports according to his employer's policies. This receipt had to be handed in a certain way, that form had to be filled out in a certain way. He said, "This is crazy. You're reducing my billable client time by eight hours a month. Here . . . I run my financial life on Mint.com. I already did this work once, for myself. Here's a one-page printout that has everything you need." Now, rather than save receipts he just orders up duplicate sets to match his expenses from SalesReceiptStore.com, a service that prints and mails receipt copies for expense reports. Then he attaches them to the one-pager from Mint.com and submits them to accounting. He's been reimbursed correctly and quickly ever since. Net/net: He gets reimbursed *and* he eliminated two hours of stupid-work per week.

in those meetings that I was excluded from started coming to me. Now I'm a consultant to the college, helping them accomplish the same kind of community building and sharing with all faculty—both full- and part-time."

Even in the most bureaucratic and hierarchical situations, there's always a work-around that will help you accomplish your goals.

## YOU NEED TO HACK

While the learn-by-hacking gene is in all of us since birth, what forces it out in our workplace is business's failure to meet more of our needs and its insistence on focusing mainly on its needs.

When company leaders talk about "productivity" and "efficiency," they're using *organizational* definitions: the fewest people accomplishing the highest output in the least amount of time at the lowest cost.

When hackers use those terms, they're referring to *personal* definitions: how I juggle all the daily demands in my life—my commitments to me, my family, my boss, my teammates, my customers, my company, my community, my dreams—with the least amount of effort, time, and hassle in ways that deliver the most value and allow me to be true to myself.

You deserve to have the tools, structures, and processes that *you* need to do your best, not just the ones the company needs to do its best. You *should and must* maintain your own view of personal productivity: the least amount of effort from you with the most value returned back to you, which keeps you doing your best. That's the only way to ensure your success as well as your contribution's largest impact.

If you're getting all that and more from your current job—great! No need to hack. But if you haven't been given the tools and processes you need, it's time to go get them or rework them. What you need to succeed is readily available, even if your boss didn't give it to you.

It's time to free your inner hacker. We'll show you how.

SIDETRIP

## WHAT COLOR IS YOUR HAT?

**White Hat** Hackers are ethical hackers. They're most often insiders who work around their own systems to improve them. Good guys.

**Gray Hat** Hackers expose vulnerabilities in systems to help make the systems better. Good guys (as long as the owners of the systems are open to tough love).

**Black Hat** Hackers attack systems for profit and fun at the expense of others or to advance an agenda. Indisputable bad guys.

# YES, THERE IS A DARK SIDE

**This book** is focused on benevolent hacks, but we cannot ignore that Black Hatters are doing evil things and giving some hacks a bad name.

These acts range from mildly bad (law firm Pillsbury Winthrop Shaw Pittman had salary cuts disclosed on blogs before some of the associates affected were told by their managers) to horribly bad (in 2008, hacker Albert Gonzalez and two Russian counterparts were charged for breaching over 130 million credit card records). In 2009, Iraqi insurgents hacked U.S. military drones using $26 software, and in 2010, Israeli soldier GI Schmo revealed his unit's secret upcoming raid to the world, including the enemy, on Facebook.

The most recent security threat report by Sophos says that unprotected data remains a top concern and that digital espionage and cybercrime are increasing. It lists examples such as Great Britain's biggest bank robbery ever, executed by hackers, and the theft of a single laptop that put 109,000 pension holders at risk. Also, one in four businesses report that malware and phishing have snuck in through their employees' use of social networking sites.

Yes, hacking has a dark side requiring constant vigilance. Acknowledge its presence, respect its power for doing harm, but never let those evildoers stop you from benevolent hacks. Make sure the White Hatters win!

# GET HACKING

Stupid rules shift the costs of work from the company onto you without delivering equal or better value back to you.

This means you pay the price for someone else's bureaucracy or, worse, for their bad decisions.

Breaking stupid rules means getting smarter results: for you, your team, and your company.

Here's how. . . .

# BREAKING STUPID RULES FOR SMART RESULTS

Get rid of everything that isn't useful, beautiful, or joyful.

—Anonymous, via viral email

## GETTING STARTED

All Nina needed was a new printer. Why wouldn't her company get it for her, and why should you care? Because her plight is exactly why we must all hack our work. At its core, her story is our story.

Nina is a teleworker who manages projects for a health care organization from her home. In the spring of 2009, her company refused to replace her color printer, even though it was on its last legs after seven years. They insisted on a black-and-white model because that could translate to a savings of about $300 per year in toner costs. Multiply that by thousands of printers throughout the company, and at first glance, that mandate makes perfect sense—cost controls are necessary in all businesses.

But nobody listened to why Nina insisted on color: The way IT set up her project management system, everyone she communicates with gets assigned a different color within their electronic exchanges. So for her paper-based files and project maps (which are required by her company to qualify for ongoing project manager certification), Nina bought her own rainbow assortment of colored highlighters and now has to manually highlight each person's contributions and changes with a different color.

Nowhere does the company's balance sheet record that it created $300 in savings by off-loading all that extra work onto Nina. Nowhere does Nina's salary or bonus or job description reflect this extra pain-in-the-ass, non-value-added work. Nowhere do corporate productivity numbers record that the company actually *decreased* Nina's personal productivity and minimized her ability to do her best work by saving itself a few hundred bucks.

This kind of destructive cost shift is more the norm than the exception. Each and every one of us has our own Nina story—where there is no tracking of all the hard and soft costs that corporate-centered processes create for and off-load onto us.

If it's not a printer, it's a regimented procedure or form or software that means more work for us but fewer costs and more control for the company.

Now that you know you were born to hack, and before we jump into the how-tos, never forget *why* you're hacking. Cost controls are just as necessary for you as they are for your company, and hacking is a way of exercising your own controls. If, like Nina, you've had enough of all those destructive cost shifts, here's how to get started.

## WHAT'S BUGGING YOU?

The first step is the easiest. You tried to get something done and how you were forced to do it ticked you off. You grumbled to yourself, "Stupid procedure," or, "Stupid meeting, stupid form," stupid this or that. Start there, with whatever's bugging you, not because it bugs you—that's not reason enough—but because you know this problem. You

## SELECTING WHAT TO HACK

1. **Select the Three Things That Drive You the Most Crazy.** You know the enemy: stupid rules, lack of common sense, and "Because I say so." Which three pain-in-the-ass tools, rules, and processes are the biggest drain on your personal productivity?

2. **Learn a Little More About Each One.** What *don't* you know about how that form or process or tool works? Why do others insist you do things that way? Who or what would be affected if you hacked a work-around?

3. **For Your First Hack, Keep It Simple.** Select your first hack for how easy it is to create your work-around. Most people should attempt more difficult hacks only with the help of a team or with some hacking experience.

4. **Start with the End in Mind: Define Success.** How will your hack change . . . your workload? your stress or frustration? your productivity? how you spend your time? What will you do with the extra time, energy, and passion now available because of your hack?

live it every day. It's one of the ways you're *supposed* to do things that bears no resemblance to common sense. You're about to change that.

## NEXT: LOOK TO YOUR LEFT, LOOK TO YOUR RIGHT

If hacking includes understanding a system well enough to take it apart and do something better with it—what's a system? Big subject, but all you need to know for hacking is one little thing: connections.

If you're going to hack a task, a process, or a tool, you need to be curious about how that thing is connected to other things. For example, if you were a Yale University student writing a paper about an idea that would eventually become FedEx, you'd look at how UPS got packages from Boston to Billings and from Berlin to Beijing. You'd study the connections between each task throughout the entire system—everything that happens between "I'd like to send a package" to "It just arrived"—and then find a way to hack it. FedEx founder and CEO Fred Smith did just that. His original innovation was to hack the system of shipping packages. He took it apart and put it back together in ways that saved money and greatly sped up how packages got from point A to point B.

Most readers of this book won't need to study entire systems as Smith did. Your most important job will be to look to your immediate left and right—to see the connections between whatever it is you've got to handle, how it was handed to you, and how you'll hand it off to others.

So if you're hacking an expense form that seems useless, first make sure you understand all the elements of the form that was handed to you and what happens to the numbers within the form after you turn it in. Same with hacking into anything related to IT: You already know the limitations of the tool you're stuck with; learn as much as you can about what it does well so your new solution doesn't lose any of that. Then think about how your boss and teammates will be affected by a new approach.

One potential danger: Better understanding of these things can sometimes lead to Stockholm syndrome, where someone who is forced to do things against his will ends up sympathizing with the perpetrator. Criminologist Nils Bejerot named this behavior when bank employees who were held hostage for six days defended their captors after they were freed, insisting that their kidnappers' cause was just. Your equivalent would be: "Oh, poor corporation. It must be tough having to secure all its IT tools from employees who would download porn all day or share secrets with competitors or . . . horror of horrors . . . not use PowerPoint. I guess I'll use their outdated legacy systems and work twice as hard as I need to because *their* work will be harder if I don't."

Don't be a victim twice: As you seek to understand the system surrounding your hack, never forget that you are the one currently being held hostage! And that wasn't a nice thing to do to you.

Look to your left. Look to your right. Understand what's connected to whatever's bugging you. Done? OK, let's start hacking. . . .

## THE TWO WAYS TO HACK

**So many ways to take back control. So little time.**

Let us help you focus your energies: There are only two broad categories for work hacks. Drawing upon tech-lingo, we call them Hard Hacks and Soft Hacks.

Hard Hacks mostly change things.

Soft Hacks mostly change working relationships.

**Hard Hacks are any changes you make to non-living systems.** They are the actions that enable you to bypass a work procedure that was designed for you to follow. Hard Hacks work around corporate-sponsored tools, to-dos, forms, and processes and create ways of doing things that work for *you* and your teammates.

Here's an example of a Hard Hack you could do easily with just your smartphone or laptop if you're on a wireless network. Hiroki, a mid-manager at an automobile-manufacturing firm, was tired of having to do meetings after the meeting with his boss to decide what should have been decided in the first meeting. Corporate culture included an unending series of "buy-in" meetings before anyone could actually do anything. And that meant everything took ten times longer than was necessary. (So this hack is focused on a procedure and will use technology as the work-around.)

Hiroki and his teammates started using instant messaging (IM) to secretly pass notes back and forth to one another during team meetings. They were able to quickly come to consensus among themselves on whatever issue was before them while their boss blabbered on and on. Then at the end of the meeting, Hiroki proposed what he knew the team had already decided. Everyone agreed—no need for the meeting after the meeting or for the meeting after that to communicate what had been decided.

What's newly exciting about Hard Hacks is that even if your hack requires much higher levels of tech know-how and tools than Hiroki's work-around, you no longer have to be a geek to do them. You can Google "how to do . . ." for almost anything and you'll be blown away by the variety and depth of solutions out there. Tons of people are posting videos, offering detailed instructions, and participating in discussion groups about all sorts of work-arounds. So if what you want to do is hack something where the technology is beyond you, have no fear! There's somebody out there who's already written instructions for non-techies.

Some additional examples of Hard Hacks:

- ▶ Corporate firewalls make it hard to move information easily among teammates? No problem: Use Gmail, Google Docs, and open source Web tools as go-betweens.
- ▶ Corporate IT supports CrackBerrys, but not your iPhone or Nokia or Droid? No problem: Hack a work-around. All the instructions you need can be found on the Internet. For example, here's one forum's post for getting Lotus Notes onto your iPhone: "I use CompanionLink to sync my Notes account to a Google account, which is then pushed to my iPhone."
- ▶ Corporate IT makes it hard to get at data you need to do your job? No problem: An alpha geek will happily help you install a program that will dump a customer database into a spreadsheet.

Let's rewind through chapters 1 and 3 to see who used Hard Hacks: Richard Saunders's hack of his bank's IT system to meet the needs of his senior execs; the trainer whose material "sucked" because she was underfunded and sent her trainees elsewhere; the university employee who sold corporate trash on eBay to fund his projects; the manager who used YouTube to get her bosses to change their minds; the team who secretly hosted internal information on outside servers. These are all examples of Hard Hacks.

As you can see, there are many types of Hard Hacks, and they vary from relatively safe to daring. But what they all have in common is that the hack creates changes in a non-living system.

**Soft Hacks are anything that changes your relationship or work agreement with another person or group—changing how they agree to operate because you intervened.**

Many Soft Hacks will feel quite natural. Even though technically they are work-arounds, Soft Hacks are the obvious things that any smart person would do to build and maximize relationships, get work done, and achieve good results.

Soft Hacks are both a little easier and trickier than Hard Hacks. They can be easier because you can often sit down with the other party and say, "Hey, can we work this out?" You can't do that with a form or a tool or a mandated process or procedure. On the other hand, Soft Hacks can be trickier because you may be messing with that person's turf. And since they revolve around people, Soft Hacks are almost always more complicated.

Soft Hacks are generally broken down into two types: **Negotiating the Deal** and **Changing the Relationship**. The former involves setting the rules up front, before actual work begins; and the latter affects relationship norms that are already in place between you and the other parties.

Courtney employed a couple of **Negotiating the Deal** hacks when her family situation suddenly changed. She had to convince her manager to let her work remotely.

The first thing she did was to offer her manager something in return—she packaged her off-site request as a way to speed up delivery dates on two of his three top-priority projects. That took about a month of preplanning and behind-the-scenes secondary negotiations with teammates and vendors before she was ready to lay out everything for her manager. It also included some reordering of the sequence of tasks to be completed. Lots of people had to agree to help her make the changes she needed to make.

She didn't get everything she wanted; eventually, Courtney and her manager settled on a compromise—three days per week working remotely and two on-site. But she got further than anyone else in her position ever had.

Other examples of Negotiating the Deal hacks:

▶ Seeking different measures for your projects.
▶ Negotiating up front on salary and benefits. We discovered that in addition to using age-old techniques, many hackers are doing their own due diligence with new tools to play hardball with their employers. For example, BrightScope. com provides detailed comparative rankings for the 401(k) plans of hundreds of companies. Hackers who found that their potential employer was not in the top quartile used data from BrightScope to forge a better deal in other areas, like base compensation and benefits.
▶ Getting an extremely tailored training and development program. Same as above; we found that many hackers went to initial interviews armed with rankings of where their firm fell in terms of training and development and used that data to get a better overall deal than they could have otherwise.

What makes each of these a hack rather than a normal relationship give-and-take is that each is a clear exception to the company's normal procedures. For example, because of her supervisory role,

Courtney's job description never offered the possibility of working remotely. She had to create the exception to the rule. And while hacks on tightly controlled areas like compensation appear to be relatively minimal, they are definitely becoming more common. It is doable, even in a down economy! Hackers everywhere are discovering that if they do enough due diligence, almost any standardized "nonnegotiable" practice can be hacked.

Your Negotiating the Deal hack assumes that you are just as special as the most senior executive at your firm. You know that behind-closed-doors deals are made for them all the time; companies make all kinds of exceptions for the people who matter. In today's not-fair-to-all workplaces, Negotiating the Deal hacks are the only way to ensure that *you* matter as much as anyone else and that you get as good a deal as anyone else.

Could this create lots of complexity for companies—lots of people like you negotiating individual and tailored deals? Absolutely. Should you care? Not one bit! Did they care when their corporate-centered designs had you working twice as hard as necessary, forced work/life stresses onto you and your family, or forced you to take on twice as much work when they laid off your teammates? Their priority is to avoid tailored deals to create assembly-line efficiencies in all their people processes. Is that *your* priority? Didn't think so.

Most Boomers we interviewed saw Negotiating the Deal hacks as having to give up something in order to get what they wanted, just as Courtney did: "If you let me work remotely, I'll increase such-and-such for you." Their approach seemed to be "You get more flies with honey than with vinegar." Millennials, however, were more in-your-face: "Why should I even have to ask for these things? It's what I need to do my job!" Many in this generation will assume that almost everything is up for negotiation. That could mean lots more acceptance of this kind of hack or that you'll have lots of competition for the few tailored deals that are done.

Some think that negotiation must be hardball back-and-forth, with both parties digging in to get their way. But negotiating can be as simple as asking to get a copy of a document emailed to you instead of faxed or requesting that you are called instead of emailed. Or it can be agreeing that in order to succeed, you will need certain questions answered before beginning each project—and if your boss doesn't have the answers, it's OK for you to ask her boss. Negotiating the Deal is setting precedents for how *you* need to work so that you can succeed and excel more often.

And that's the point. Too many times, the deal you're handed ensures the company's success, but not yours. Hacking back ensures that you get to do your best.

The other kind of Soft Hack involves **Changing the Relationship**:

- ▶ Organizing anything to improve morale, from safe approaches like sponsoring a company softball team to more daring approaches like confronting a toxic boss with your own bottom-up survey.
- ▶ Bypassing the formal 360° feedback or performance systems to get a good person promoted or a bad person disciplined.
- ▶ For those with great bosses, this hack is for you, too: Many hackers said that they partnered with their manager, who helped keep their hacks "under the radar" and provided "air cover" protection if those in power ever found out.
- ▶ Reaching out to your own social network instead of to the people assigned to you by the company.

All Soft Hacks involve social engineering, which is just a clever way of saying that everybody has needs, wants, and desires that can be leveraged with positive or negative reinforcement. If any of that makes you queasy or feels like manipulation, get over it! Remember, your company is hacking you right now. What do you think rewards and recognition are all about? Yup, social engineering.

A classic example comes from Josh's time at Microsoft. He was a blue badge worker—a contractor. The red badgers were full-time employees, which included a crucial reward: stock options. Every midmorning, those red badgers would cluster over coffee to discuss that day's stock price. They'd chortle about how much richer they'd soon be, lording it over the blue badgers. The social pressure worked. Those blue contract workers were constantly putting in more effort, hoping they, too, could become one of those well-rewarded red badgers. And Microsoft benefited from all that extra effort, while only rarely elevating blue badgers to red status.

Sound familiar? Even if it's not as competitive or obvious, most companies have some version of red vs. blue social engineering.

We're just showing you how to hack back—how to level this portion of the playing field.

More important, know that it's called social *engineering* for a reason. Most of us manage the give-and-take of our relationships in a knee-jerk way as situations arise. Hacks that change your relationships are about being more proactive in thinking through how those relationships can help you do your best.

One final, crucial note about all Soft Hacks: If you rework any relationship to improve your output, you've got to deliver the goods! Hackers thrive in meritocracies, which means having the capabilities to back up your work-arounds with real value. Otherwise you'll be using others for your own gain. In hacker's lingo, that's "being a dick." Don't be a dick.

## POP QUIZ AND A FEW QUICK TIPS

Remember Matt, the new hire in chapter 1 who created his own performance assessment tool and got his company to agree to use it? Quiz time: Did Matt employ a Hard Hack or a Soft Hack?

Trick question! He used both. Redesigning his company's performance assessment tool was a Hard Hack—he changed a non-living thing. But he got it implemented through Soft Hacks. First he used

LinkedIn, a social networking tool, to find someone to help him improve his hack. Then, prepared with a negotiation strategy as well as the backing of some of his teammates, he went to HR and his boss and won a new negotiated deal.

The most effective hacks often combine hard and soft approaches. Examples from what you've read already in chapter 3: Sean's negotiations with the CIO to off-load his team onto HR and then working around the CIO with his team's prototype; LeeAnne Del Rio's use of a Web site to change relationships between part-time and full-time teachers. These are examples of Hard Hacks combined with Soft Hacks.

Why does this work so well? Most often because you're making it easier for them—all they have to do is say OK to a fix that solves their own problem.

**Hacking Quick Tip 1: Use Hard and Soft Hacks in Combination.** Even if you're hacking a non-living thing, you are also changing somebody's world. Somebody owns that form or process. If you can, work with those who will be impacted. Or, as Matt did, seek the support of others so you don't go it alone. The biggest enemy to a successful hack is catching others by surprise. Many of the most effective hackers said that their immediate supervisor was in on their hack. The more people you can loop into your hack and empower by your hack, the better.

**Hacking Quick Tip 2: Hard Hacks Are Often Bold Acts.** Hard Hacks have the potential to create the biggest shifts in power in the shortest period of time. This is because many of them can be scaled—replicated by lots of others—and because they're often easier to keep underground for a longer period of time. This makes Hard Hacks the most effective, but also the most risky. Bosses don't expect anyone to question their system, so redesigning your work tools can be like telling the emperor he needs new clothes.

**Hacking Quick Tip 3: Pick Battles You Can Win.** After trying unsuccessfully for months to get a color printer, Nina finally decided to take another tack. Having proven herself to be a vital resource to the company, she used a Negotiating the Deal hack to reprioritize her workload, more than making up for the silly extra duties of high-lighting printouts.

You now have the basics for getting started. In chapter 5, we'll go deeper into breaking stupid rules for smart results—how to build your own hacker's toolkit and the five hacks you definitely should try.

FASTHACKS

## WORK-AROUNDS FROM THE FIELD

**How Techies Negotiate for Time Off** from Jessica: "I recently worked for a company that was stingy with time-off allocations but demanded a lot of overtime. What made my situation worse was that while I was putting in all that overtime, my supervisor worked just enough to get by and always took off as soon as our boss left for the day.

"I knew that all our work involved the same network. Since I was in charge of the network, I wrote a script to send me an email every time my supervisor logged in and out. I wrote the same script to track my log-in and log-out times. I imported all the data into a spreadsheet and could soon accurately compare my sixty-plus-hour workweeks with my supervisor's forty-plus-hour weeks.

"Later that year, I met with both my supervisor and our boss and told them I was going to take an extra week over Christmas holiday to visit my in-laws overseas. After the yelling had ended, I handed them my spreadsheet comparing my supervisor's work hours and mine. Instead of the additional week I had requested, they gave me ten additional days off.

*(continued)*

"Upon my return, I was treated with much greater respect, and my employment with them lasted until I chose to end it."

**Even Apples Need Hacking** from Lucas: "I emailed [CEO] Steve Jobs instead of following the standard chain of command at Apple to address coding issues with a customer interface. We had been having this problem for several months, and we were getting nowhere. Needless to say, the problem was miraculously addressed the next day."

# 5

# FIVE HACKS EVERYONE SHOULD DO

Behind all this, some great happiness is hiding.

—Yehuda Amichai, Israel's greatest modern poet

## FOR BEST RESULTS: BUILD YOUR OWN TOOLKIT

This is the point at which lots of hacking newbies lose their way.
Most want to jump immediately to "How do I get my company to be
OK with my hack? How do I get buy-in?" That actually comes much
later. Before then, it's more important to become one with *why* you
must hack and how to become a truly *benevolent* hacker. (To drive
that home, if you're seeking advice on getting the company to be OK
with your hack, don't look for it until chapter 11.)

Instead, focus first on building your own toolkit, because that's
the foundation for almost all your hacks—whether your company is
on board or not.

Your own toolkit. What's that? And why is it important?

If your goal is to control your own destiny, you'll need to identify
any tools provided by your employer that do not work for you and

replace them with your own. You are going to have to wean yourself from being locked into any one company's infrastructure. If you're willing to do that, you'll find that you're able to manage work flow better, get a lot more done faster, and focus more on adding value rather than just checking off to-dos—all because you worked in ways that were best *for you*.

Every company has their own procedures, processes, and ways of doing things. They also use specific software applications and devices to run all those procedures. In most (not all) cases, you don't *really* have to use those apps, devices, or procedures. There are tons of other options available, often for free.

So by toolkit, we mean your own portable infrastructure—a suite of apps, a collection of devices, and ways of doing things that *work best for you*, that can be used in different workplaces and different situations throughout your career. Your goal, now and always, should be to scan the horizon for new and better ways to support yourself—in how you communicate, manage projects, build teams and communities, and more. This is a second-millennium necessity for proactively managing your career.

Of course, you'll always be locked into *some* of your employer's infrastructure, but if you develop your own toolkit and keep building it, you'll be amazed to discover how much of theirs you can bypass. And the great news is that because user-centered tools are becoming de rigueur (everywhere outside of work), you should be able quickly and easily to find whatever you need.

Build your own toolkit and take it with you everywhere!

## DETAILED TOOLKIT ADVICE FROM AN ALPHA HACKER

How should you get started? Many hackers gave us tips to pass along, but one stood out because he explained why each toolset and each step in the process was so damned important.

Gary Koelling is director of emerging platforms at Best Buy, the

# TOP FIVE HACKS WE'D RECOMMEND THAT EVERYONE DO

**Hard Hacks** mostly change things.
**Soft Hacks** mostly change working relationships.

Here's an ideal mix for most people. Use your portable hacker's toolkit to make them happen.

1. **Hack Your New Hire Process. (**Soft**)** The best results you'll ever get with a Negotiating the Deal hack will be as a new hire. Ensure that your relationship with the firm benefits you as much as it does them.

2. **Hack One Small Thing That Saps Your Energy. (**Hard**)** Cut one step out of a procedure through a work-around and improve your own efficiency. Make it small enough to guarantee success. This quick win will boost your confidence for more hacks.

3. **Hack the Start of Every New Project. (**Combine Hard and Soft**)** Each project is a new opportunity to ensure a successful career. Begin by seeking clearer goals; get more useful project information; ensure access to anyone and anything you need. Build on each successful hack with bigger, bolder hacks.

4. **Hack One Big Thing That Destroys Your Efficiency. (**Hard**)** Now that you're more experienced, tackle the most stupid procedure or tool that the company has built that saps your efficiency. You will get high praise from your boss's bosses, because they'll think you're producing twice as much within their rules!

*(continued)*

> **5. Hack to Make the World a Better Place. (Hard)**
> Volunteer your time, energy, and talents on someone
> else's Hard Hack that will improve all workplaces.
> Change a form, a process, or a tool, and share the
> hack with the world through public forums such as
> HackingWork.com.

global electronics retailer. Gary's hack was to build BlueShirt Nation (BSN), which is a secure social network for about one hundred thousand Best Buy employees.

Think of BSN as Facebook inside a company. At the same time employees are getting to know one another—yes, they even post pictures of their cats—they're also sharing best practices among stores, answering customers' questions, and chatting about new ways to serve customers. As Gary put it, "A company's culture cannot be disseminated to the masses as policy from above. BSN is a tool we use to create that for ourselves, sharing across hierarchies and departments. Our customers can feel the difference."

But what makes Gary invaluable to you as a resource are not the specifics of BlueShirt Nation, but the hard-won lessons he learned in building his own toolkit before creating BSN for Best Buy. It's all about serving the company *and* one's own future at the same time.

**Gary Koelling on Tools:** "Corporate-supplied tools should be avoided at all costs and as much as possible: If you're asking yourself should you use your company's network and tools instead of building your own toolkit, the answer is 'No.' Of course you're free to try that, but you're also free to stick needles in your eyes. It's really up to you."

Now that you know where he's coming from, here's how Gary would suggest getting started on your own toolkit: "Download Free-Mind or any other free mind-mapping software. You can map a customer problem, a work flow, a project, anything—you'll be amazed at how much clearer your thinking becomes. Download the Web browser Firefox, then explore all the cool add-ons you can install. . . . Now, sign up for a free Basecamp account. It's a forum, a to-do list, a whiteboard, a file repository, and more—and it's dead simple to use. Use Campfire or Dimdim to do meetings without being in the same room as your co-conspirators. These are specialized virtual meeting tools—but often Google's GTalk or a similar instant message client will suffice, or Adium for those of you lucky enough to ride Macs. You don't need all the expensive videoconferencing/telepresence tools companies are hawking these days."

If you're unfamiliar with these tools (or find your eyes glazing over from too much geek-speak), Google them to learn more or browse the articles at LifeHacker.com or similar sites. There are many online resources for sharing hacks that help you to take charge of your life.

Almost anything you need can be found on the Net. Is your company too restrictive with hard drive or in-box space? Or you want to maintain files that you don't want seen by the IT police? Instructables.com has a step-by-step video on how to use your Gmail account as a free 7 GB external drive. Multiple Gmail accounts mean essentially that you have at your disposal unlimited amounts of free external storage space.

Super-important: Remember that technology changes continuously. By the time we go to press, some of what's listed here will be outdated. And since there's so much more to hacking than knowing technology, we consciously decided to leave more techno-stuff out of this book than we put in.

Always remember that technology isn't the point—building a portable toolkit that works for you is. And don't forget that techno-tools are just the enablers, things that will help you take control of your own destiny. Is your own techno-toolkit important? Yes. Do you need to be a geek to build one? No.

Constantly use your own wikis and blogs and tools like those Gary has mentioned, because at some point all the comments and inter-linked items that are posted will be extremely useful in proving the value of your projects to your boss's boss. And here's the best part: Most everything you need is either free or very cheap. For next to nothing you can build an extremely personalized toolkit, just for you, that goes with you whenever you leave.

We asked Gary what people should do if their company blocks these sites or prohibits these tools. "Well, you've got to ask yourself: How much is my own success worth? Is it worth a few bucks to hack around the company network? A wireless broadband card runs about $60 a month. If you want to share that cost with others, you can plug said card into a Cradlepoint unit and create a wireless network in your little neck of the cube forest for about $100."

**On Partnering with Your Company:** We've spoken with enough non-hackers to know what questions come next: "Isn't there any way to stay more within the corporate rules?" "How would you build your toolkit so it meshes more completely with the company's preexisting tools and processes?"

"You don't," Gary says matter-of-factly. "The main thing you need to accept, and this is what drives many midmanagers bug-shit crazy, is that most companies design things the wrong way. They focus on building things they can manage, control, and regulate. That's *corporate*-centered design. Your success, including a successful partnership with your company, will actually come from being *user* centered and by just paying attention.

"Stay with me—it's not as counterintuitive as that may seem. When Steve Bendt and I built BlueShirt Nation, we had a single little problem we were trying to solve: Get our employees to tell us what customers were telling them. That was it. We had no authority requiring people to join the network or use certain tools, let alone answer our specific questions. The 'authority' we had was to choose how we were going to approach the problem. We used open source, open standard software and principles. Then we watched and listened. The users told us where the project should go from there.

"As you can imagine, no one with a corporate mind-set, using corporate resources, would have approved our approach. We couldn't answer, 'What's the long-term vision?' or, 'When will it scale?' or the one that drives everything: 'What's the ROI?'"

What Gary's advocating is madness, right? No. . . . Actually, it's a brilliant strategy that nearly every hacker we interviewed employs.

He notes wisely, "Our bosses are no different from yours. They focus on results. The key is to start delivering results—in our case, being more focused on the customer—*before* getting involved in all those ROI discussions. That's where being user centered comes in. You do things on the cheap, you learn fast, you incorporate what you learn from users fast, and you deliver real results faster than those corporate-centered designs could have. So approvals end up being based on what you've already done, not on what you're planning to do. And the forbidden work-around is easily forgotten because you've delivered results that made the boss look good."

## A Few Last Tips for Building Your Own Toolkit

Results matter. Hacking transgressions will be forgiven if you deliver the goods faster and better than if you did it the "right" way. Far more important than worrying about whether your boss will be OK with you using your own toolkit is learning how to hack so you deliver results up front, *before* the other conversations even begin.

Finally, here's the really cool upside to small, cheap, and fast hacks: Most people around you won't try it. Most people would rather plan than act. Know what that means? Using your own toolkit to hack fast and deliver fast results is a big, sustainable advantage that will serve you throughout your career.

## WORK-AROUNDS FROM THE FIELD

**Be the Note Taker** from midmanager Alex: "I work for one of the world's largest megacorps. My hack had a five-year run and was extremely simple and low-risk. I volunteered to be the note taker and occasional moderator for key cross-functional and global operational planning sessions. What that meant was that I was able to contact and coordinate with all the groups and individuals that my bosses didn't know, think about, or believe they needed to care about. I maintained hundreds of covert and underground relationships and used those relationships to place what wasn't discussed—but should have been—into the meeting notes. It's all about relationships. Simple. Obvious. But just doesn't happen without hacks in most big companies."

**Entrepreneurial Carpet Cleaners Hack, Too** from Thomas, a retired and successful business owner: "For twenty years I was a manager for a European airline. We hit tough times after 9/11, so I took a buyout, came to America, and invested in a franchised carpet-cleaning service. The cleaning tools they provided were good, but not as good as they could be. So I modified the standard sprayer to get more coverage, added a Teflon piece to aid in moving over rough surfaces, and changed the suction tube to shorten the suction distance and increase the amount of crud that the machine picked up. I also brewed up my own mixes that get stains out better than what the company provided. Redesigning these tools and processes has become a unique advantage, as my competitors are competing against the way I'm *supposed* to be doing everything."

## FIVE HACKS EVERYONE SHOULD DO

Now, all that can be reduced to the essentials, the five hacks that are likely to be the ideal mix for most people. (See SmartStart box on pages 47–48 for more.)

1. If you can, the best place to start hacking is as a new hire— before you officially join the team and throughout the new hire process. It's much easier to discuss tailoring things just for you at the outset than to try to back into them later. These are Negotiating the Deal hacks: adjusting what your accountabilities will be, how you'll be measured, how you'll be accountable, and to whom. Hard Hacks—hacking tools and systems—come later.

2. Then comes KISS: Keep it simple and small. After a month or two, hack one little thing that keeps sapping your energy. It could be texting during a stupid meeting or asking a teammate how she avoids stupid stuff. You're not looking to change the entire system; your main goal at this point is to accomplish a quick win—boosting your confidence for bigger and bolder hacks. This is the first place your toolkit will come in handy. Depending on your hack, it could be using your own email or IM service instead of the company's or using your own wiki to organize your ideas your way before importing them into a structure that works for the company. Just keep it small enough so you can do it with very little effort.

3. Always watch for the biggest opportunity for new hacks: the start of every new project. Each one can be treated separately. . . . Negotiate new measures here; arrange different information flows there; change access to decision makers or customers or other teammates. Reach into your toolkit for better ways than the company provided to

communicate and better ways to organize your ideas and share them with others. Depending on your job, you'll get anywhere from half a dozen to scores of new projects every year. Treat each one as an opportunity to do an incremental hack, and by the end of a year you will have had a major impact!

4. Now, with experience under your belt, go for the big one. Hack the most stupid procedure that not only saps your energy but destroys the efficiency and effectiveness of so many around you. Be daring. Be bold. Use as much of your own toolkit as you can. Change the tools and infrastructure that the company simply refuses to change on its own. Share what you've done with as many teammates as you can so they, too, can work around the company's stupid-work. Not every hacker gets to this point, but if you can, you will truly be saving business from itself and making everyone's lives a lot better.

5. Finally, pay it forward. Make the world a better place by sharing what you've learned through a blog or some other media that will reach people you don't even know. Somewhere, somebody is struggling with the same stupid thing. They need help, and you've got the experience they need. Volunteer your time and energy to make all workplaces just a little better.

# DO NO HARM

> May the forces of evil become confused on the
> way to your house.
>
> —George Carlin, the ultimate fool's fool

## AN ETHICAL GUIDE TO DOING GOOD, DOING WELL, AND DOING NO EVIL

A trolley is running out of control down a track. In its path are five people who have been tied to the track. Fortunately, you can flip a switch that will lead the trolley down a different track to safety. Unfortunately, there is a single person tied to that other track. Should you flip the switch?

That's an example of a classic ethical dilemma created by Philippa Ruth Foot, one of the founders of contemporary virtue ethics as well as Oxfam International. Trolleys too old school for you? How about these twenty-first-century dilemmas...

Flash mob hacks are becoming mainstream. This is where disruptive protests are staged, but the event is ephemeral. The real power is in posting it on YouTube as a way to instantly mobilize global opinions. An Oakland, California, Whole Foods recently came to a standstill as carts clogged every aisle and a flash mob sang about the store's health care practices. In May 2010, the Westin St. Frances hotel in San Francisco was stormed by a mob singing "Boycott, boycott . . . Worker's rights are hot . . . This is a bad, bad hotel" to a Lady Gaga tune.

Protests have been around forever, but the rules are changing. Dilemma: If your manager or company is holding you back, would you be more effective negotiating with them directly or letting a YouTube video speak for you?

Another opportunity as ethical dilemma: As we went to press, the Diaspora project was building the first open-source social network tool designed to be owned by individuals. If it is successful, soon you and everyone else can own the exact terms under which your Twitter and Facebook accounts, or any of your other content is used, accessed, or seen. No more need for a centralized authority—hmm, who thinks that will stay *outside* the workplace?

## WHOSE PRODUCTIVITY COMES FIRST?

Benevolent hackers live by a strict moral code. Unfortunately, most non-hackers view ethics through such a different lens, they just don't see hacking as an ethical behavior. Here, we'll try to build some common ground and useful ways to examine the good that's already happening.

"Hacking your work is breaking the rules, and it's wrong" is flat-out wrong because it denies and invalidates that so many good, hard-working people are forced into hacks just to get their work done.

We get a little closer to a workable discussion when we consider moral dilemmas like the trolley scenario. You're thrown into a situation—do stupid, non-value-added work or hack a work-around and risk pissing off your boss—and you a experience a moral dilemma that feels like a no-win situation.

But that's a victim's approach to work—damned if you do, damned if you don't. So that's not really a valuable lens either.

The best lens to use to understand the dynamic of what's going on is the classic comedy routine "Who's on First?" When Bud Abbott says, "Who," it's perfectly clear in his mind what that means: the first baseman's name. When Lou Costello says, "Who?" he knows he's asking a question. They're in a conversation that is constructed so they're both right, but neither is listening to the other!

Productivity . . . efficiency . . . cost cutting . . . Whose view comes first?

Nina kicked off this question for us in chapter 4 when she needed a certain kind of printer to do the work required of her, but the company refused so they could save $300. In a discussion of productivity, efficiency, and cost cutting, whose view is right? Is it the company's—the fewest people accomplishing the highest output in the least amount of time at the lowest cost? Or is it the individual's—juggling all the demands on me with the least amount of effort, time, and hassle, in ways that deliver the most value, and in ways where the company's cost-saving efforts are not off-loaded onto me by increasing my workload?

As in "Who's on First?" both views are right. That paradox *must* be considered when discussing the ethics of hacking work.

Here's a common social hack in today's world: texting. A bunch of 'tween-aged girls are in a movie theater and they're *not* talking (an accepted social norm for that setting). But their hack is to chat throughout the entire movie by texting each other silently. The Boomer couple behind them gets annoyed—not so much at their behavior, but because texting is not a Boomer norm—and asks them to stop. Whose ethical standard should prevail?

Same dilemma in a business setting: A manager who can make everybody attend his meeting is doing what he always does—running it in a way that no one finds useful. The attendees ignore his presentation and are busy texting on their smartphones. Whose ethical standard should prevail—the boss's, who feels he's entitled to their attention and respect because of his position and the importance of what he has to say, or the meeting hackers', who can't afford to have their time wasted?

Benevolent hackers are being extremely ethical when they hack because they need to be more personally efficient and productive than circumstances allow them to be. When they create ways to be more efficient, everybody wins: the boss, the company, the customer. . . . No ethical dilemma—just hack!

**Come Together! Both Sides Are Right.** The real problem surrounding work hacks is that people who disagree aren't talking to each other. And only those discussions that examine the potential good created by hacking, as well as the potential downside, will create a common, sustainable, and enforceable code of ethics.

Throughout the rest of this book, we'll lay out what to talk about in those conversations: what's broken now that needs to be fixed, what's ahead that will need to be addressed, how the rules have changed for both bosses and the workforce, and more.

Until those discussions bear fruit, this chapter can serve as your ethical compass. We've interviewed hundreds of hackers, searching for how they determined the difference between a benevolent hack and a malicious one.

**Here are the ten commandments of ethical workplace hacks.**

## HACK THESE COMMANDMENTS

**T**he ten commandments listed in this chapter are just a starter kit, a distillation of hundreds of interviews. They did not come from any mountaintop. Hack them! Change them. Eliminate some, add others. Make them your own. Post the results.

As hackers, here's what we know for sure: The wisdom of the crowd—you—will develop something more workable for more people than we could possibly deliver.

# 1. THERE'S REALLY ONLY ONE COMMANDMENT: BE COOL

If you're not being cool, people will kick you out—literally or emotionally. Hackers believe that if you don't know whether or not you're being cool . . . well, then you probably aren't.

(Hackers are not big on articulating their philosophy or ethics. You either get it or you don't.)

Being a hacker isn't about you or your ego—at least not if you're any good—but rather about doing your best work, having fun, and improving things for everybody. While you shouldn't break the law, there are always ways to bend the rules to make things better or productive work-arounds to achieve the results that your employers demand when they don't supply the needed tools or support.

Hackers also have a rule for being cool: Don't be an asshole.

To hackers, the "Be cool, don't be an asshole" rule is useful precisely because it's vague and incomplete. If you know that what you're doing is cool, good. Keep doing it. If you're not sure, whatever hack you're considering probably is not a good idea.

Most hackers really didn't want us to get more detailed than that. But since we knew you would like a little less vagueness, we pressed for more specifics. We've embellished upon being cool and added nine more commandments simply to address some of the concerns we've heard.

Being cool is actually pretty simple: Follow what Robert Fulghum laid out his 1986 book, *All I Really Need to Know I Learned in Kindergarten*. Some of his advice:

▶ Share everything.
▶ Play fair.
▶ Don't hit people.
▶ Put things back where you found them.
▶ Clean up your own mess.

- ► Say you're sorry when you hurt somebody.
- ► Watch for traffic, hold hands, and stick together.

Everything you need to know to be an ethical hacker, you learned in kindergarten.

To round out what it means to be cool, throw in the universal truths Don Miguel Ruiz prescribed in his book *The Four Agreements*:

- ► Be impeccable with your word.
- ► Don't take anything personally.
- ► Don't make assumptions.
- ► Always do your best.

And if you still need more, check out Stephen Covey's *The 7 Habits of Highly Effective People*.

All of that adds up to being cool.

If you hack and you are being cool, you are building a better future. You are living the future, where one person truly can make a difference, where personal efficiency and productivity are now embedded within organizational efficiencies, where all workplaces can be much more amazing places to be. Cool hackers know that transparently sharing and debating and showing what needs to change, while difficult, will *always* lead us to a better future.

## 2. TRY NON-HACKING FIRST

There's an expression: To a carpenter with a hammer, every problem looks like a nail. Never hack needlessly just because hacking is now in your toolkit. Lots of problems can be solved without hacks.

## 3. DO NO HARM

That does *not* mean don't ruffle feathers. If you hack, you will most likely upset someone. "Do no harm" means don't do anything to a system that would stop others from using it exactly the way it was supposed to be used. But at the same time, when you use that system, it now works a lot better for you. You've improved it. Some examples:

- If you're hacking an expense report, don't do anything that would prevent others from safely, securely following corporate's rules. And don't cheat on the numbers you submit!
- If you're texting in a stupid meeting instead of paying attention to the presenter, don't *dis* or gossip about the presenter. Focus on getting work done, and save the playground stuff for after hours.
- If you're jumping over IT's firewall, don't do anything that would prevent anyone who doesn't wish to hack from using the system exactly as IT intended.
- Don't hack for any of the seven deadly sins. (No porn, no greed or hoarding, no revenge or wrath, no lack of diligence or getting out of virtuous work, no enhancing your own vanity.)
- The most common hacks involve moving information differently from the dictates of an approved process and connecting with people in ways outside of how the hierarchy mandates. Never use information or relationships in a way that will make it harder for you or your teammates to do your best work.

Hacks that do no harm must deliver useful improvements in your own efficiency and effectiveness *without* damaging the company's ability to reap ongoing organizational efficiencies. (Otherwise, it's not benevolent hacking—it's stealing, for yourself and from others.) One of the keys to successfully doing no harm is to start small and keep it simple. Focus on small improvements in your and your teammates' daily lives and build from there.

## 4. NEVER COMPROMISE OTHER PEOPLE'S INFORMATION

Until the heads of IT figure out that your personal efficiency matters *as much as* their rules and security, jumping over firewalls and all related hacks are likely to keep growing as the most common workplace hack. Until IT starts working *with* you, all your benevolent hacks must maintain the highest levels of integrity in four ways:

- ▶ NEVER maintain or store customer data outside of firewalls or place such information outside the firewall in any way that compromises your ability to maintain its security.
- ▶ NEVER maintain or store corporate intellectual property outside of firewalls or place it outside the firewall in any way that compromises your ability to keep it secure. Managers will tell you that you could never keep it as secure as the company can. Unfortunately, most of the time that's just blowing smoke. (To alpha geeks, most corporate systems are as secure as Swiss cheese.) But the risk is still there, and if you screw up, it could cost you more than your job. Here's the advice we heard from hackers everywhere: If you feel you can keep it secure, hack. If you have any doubts, don't.
- ▶ NEVER share customer information or corporate intellectual property with anyone who isn't authorized to have it.
- ▶ TRIPLE-CHECK your work. Continuously review your hack to be sure the warnings above are maintained.

If your hack cannot maintain the highest levels of integrity in these four ways, it is probably inappropriate, illegal, or worse.

## 5. PLAY WELL WITH OTHERS

If your hack is not malicious, you should be able to share it with others. Do so. Build a team. Bring together people with different skills.

Whenever possible, seek support from your manager. Remember, the purpose of hacking work is to do your best—and having a strong team behind you is a great way to start.

## 6. PAY IT FORWARD

You have hacked. You benefited from that hack. Share the benefits and the how-tos with the world. As long as you maintain all the other commandments—like protecting people's and the company's identities and never sharing actual customer data or corporate intellectual property, and so forth—share as much as you can about your hack. Post what you did on blogs, in tweets, everywhere you can. Hackers believe that true transparency and the democratization of information will always serve the highest purpose. Pay the benefits forward to the world—lots of people would love to know what you know. And they'll pay you back by sharing their hacks with you.

## 7. THE LAW OF ATTRACTION WORKS

We've seen this law in action a lot recently: Videos on YouTube get viewed millions of times, are showcased and discussed on mainstream media, and create career breakout moments for some and lots of eye candy for all. For a moment, let's put aside the valid concerns that too much of this is dumbing down our global IQ. What matters here is that, applied to hacking, the law of attraction works:

- ▶ Ideas compete with one another for attention and application. Make your hack attention-worthy enough and application-worthy enough, and your hack *will* find an audience large enough to beat back corporate stupidity—and perhaps pay you for it, too!
- ▶ Share that you are trying to respect both non-hackers' and hackers' codes of ethics, and you will attract and bring

together people on both sides of this issue—achieving more change faster and gaining respect as a thought leader.

► Resources get attracted. Hack a better solution and resources, and others will find you. Nothing begets success like success.

► Pay it forward, and people you don't know will pay it back to you. Whatever you put into your hack will be attracted back to you.

## 8. BE TRUE TO YOURSELF

If you were *not* born to hack, embrace who you are. Pass this book on to someone else and follow whatever rules work for you. Conversely, if you're the kind of person who just has to take things apart and put them back together again, consider hacking as a profession! There are lots of White Hat agencies, consulting firms, and entrepreneurs that would love to have you on their team.

## 9. TALENT IS OVERRATED

That's a book title by Geoff Colvin, a senior editor at *Fortune* magazine. His premise: Practice, hard work, and perseverance—if properly analyzed and incorporated into new daily routines—help you achieve greatness.

While talent certainly is critical, and some tech skills certainly can help, most hackers do great work only through a commitment to continuous self-improvement, deliberate practice, and doing what they're passionate about.

How do you become a great benevolent hacker? Practice, practice, practice!

## 10. HACKING CAN BE A JOURNEY OF SELF-DISCOVERY

What really matters to you? How do you define doing your best? What do you stand for? How much are you willing to sacrifice and compromise to keep your job? How much is too much compromise and sacrifice?

Think back to where we began this chapter: ethical dilemmas. Follow that throughout this book: What's currently good and right to benevolent hackers is bad and wrong to some others. Another dilemma.

As human beings, anytime we live with an ethical dilemma and work through it until we make our own deeply personal decision—we grow. We learn more about ourselves, our values, our behaviors, and our beliefs.

If you choose to go there, hacking can teach you a lot about yourself.

Or . . . it can just make life and work more fun. Nothing deeper than that. Having fun is being cool, too.


## WHERE DO YOU FALL IN THIS MORALITY PLAY?

Every hack, as well as the actions of those who would oppose it, is a battle for business's soul—to redefine or to maintain the status quo.

For example, take Caroline, the volunteer coordinator at a major nonprofit organization: "I was in charge of the volunteer recognition program, but of course I was given no budget. I was also the person who opened the mail. One day I came across a letter for my executive director saying he'd won two $25 gift cards to a restaurant because he filled out some survey. He was making six figures and was an arrogant, sexist, tyrannical jerk. So I sent the gift cards to two volunteers of the month, saying they were from our organization. That simple act meant so much. They felt valued! I still feel a little guilty, but I know I did the right thing."

We see her as a hero. Her hack created a budget where there was none and recognized those who toiled hard for their organization—enthusiastic volunteers to whom a $25 gift card meant a lot.

Yet to some she's a thief: "She's stealing, plain and simple."

But at what point does underresourcing the Carolines of the world

# BENEVOLENT OR OVER THE EDGE?

**W**here's the line between benevolent hacks and ones that
go too far? Use the ten commandments of ethical hacking to
evaluate these:

**Big Savings from Locked Doors** from David: "A few years ago I
worked for an insurance company in their employee relations
department. Due to pay grade restrictions, two of my staffers
couldn't have locks on their doors. That benefit did not come
with their salary level. And yet because they handled confidential
employee records, these two had to spend a half hour at the
end of each day taking their documents and electronic files to a
secured location and then another half hour retrieving them the
next day. So I ignored company policy, put locks on their doors,
and saved them and the company ten man-hours per week."

**Clairvoyance** from Maria, a midlevel programmer who was tired
of suffering under a glass ceiling: "I put an email filter onto the
firewall to automatically bcc: me any mail with my name in it
that did not include me in the address list. This meant that any

also become stealing—when does "Do more with less" cross the line
into stealing time and energy from our families and personal lives
and add tons of unnecessary stress instead of supplying us with what
we need to do our jobs?

These are highly destructive cost shifts. At what point does the
fact that there is no tracking of all the hard and soft costs that are
off-loaded onto the workforce—creating business profits with no
paper trail of the real costs—become just plain wrong and an ethical
dilemma?

When we admit how dysfunctional many of business's current

email that was about me, but not to me, was also sent to me without anyone knowing. This way I was able to head off two HR issues by knowing about them before HR came to talk to me. With that inside intelligence, I prevented one staff reduction and turned around one business unit's concerns by presenting the solution before anyone had a chance to inform me that there was a problem." (Obviously this was a very technical hack, but it's a perfect example of what can be done with a little specialized knowledge or with a few how-to queries on Google.)

**Keeping My Phone** from Ajit, a midmanager in an insurance firm: "My company has Microsoft Exchange server for email, which only supports Outlook, except for BlackBerrys—which is a huge pain in the ass. BlackBerrys don't have the built-in tools I need for my job. No iPhones or Sidekicks, either, which is how most of us get our work done. So I run scripts [an external tool] to check the Exchange server for mail and then have it forwarded to my *real* email account on Gmail." (Curious how to do this yourself? Google "how to forward Outlook to Gmail on X," where "X" is the make and model of your phone. Tutorials will abound.)

practices are, we begin to see new truths, new moralities, new possibilities. When we openly discuss how much mediocrity, stupidity, and silly SOPs (standard operating procedures) are forced upon us, we begin to see the wisdom of hacking.

## YOU ARE JUST THE LEADER WE NEED NOW

Recent economic meltdowns are merely a symptom of an entire system going through cascade failure. "Help me!" it seems to cry. "Reboot me. Somebody save me from myself before I kill again."

You are just the kind of leader we need at this moment of change. We need you to fix business *at your level*—from your cubicle, laptop, or mobile phone; from your workstation, forklift, countertop, delivery truck, or sales or service or supervisory role; from your head, heart, and hands—one small bad act at a time.

# WHOA

Benevolent hacking wouldn't be
necessary if the design of work
didn't suck so bad—
and it's getting suckier every day.

Here's what is broken now,
what will be hitting you soon,
and that which should not be ignored.

# 7

# WHAT'S BROKEN NOW

The beatings will continue until morale
improves.

—Current approach to work design

## WHY HACKING WORK IS EXPLODING

We recently conducted a workshop on change in hard-hit Detroit.
Every manager there had close friends and family members who
had been laid off in the past month. Attempting to illustrate how
everyone's future is now in their own hands, we told the story from
chapter 1—how twenty-four-year-old Matt helped shape his job and
his career by redesigning how his performance would be assessed.
The howls of protest were deafening! "That kid just doesn't get it! He's
going to have to shut up and conform if he wants to keep his job."

Afterward, one attendee passionately wanted to set us straight
on how the real .world worked. "One of my teammates is a single
mom and works one weekend a month as a U.S. Army reservist,"
she said. "When it came time for her performance review, our boss
told her, 'I'm tired of these motherhood and American pie excuses! If

you expect to keep your job, you're going to have to put in a lot more hours.' The economy didn't do that—that's how performance reviews have always been done where I work and every place I know of. Do you think that kid is gonna get a job at any of our companies? He'd have to conform."

Unfortunately, we hear plenty of stories like this one.

The next week we attended TED, one of the premier technology conferences in the world. Elbow to elbow with the likes of Bill Gates and Jeff Bezos, we chatted over coffee with an executive in charge of all of Asia for a mega–consumer products company. We mentioned to this executive that many frontline workers were forced to hack around ridiculous restrictions imposed by their IT departments. "Tell me about it," he moaned. "For security reasons, mine won't let me use a flash drive in my laptop. I'm not supposed to transfer work files unless I do it under their scrutiny. So I went to a local electronics store and bought a $25 device that lets me transfer files anyway."

How absurd is that? This guy is in charge of the company's operations across an entire continent, he's hanging with the titans of technology, and his company treats him like a two-year-old who can't be trusted with his toys.

During a recent plane ride, we sat next to Juliana, a senior official for Medicare. With health care so much in the news lately, we decided to ask her about the impact of medical tourism. To our surprise, she had never heard of it. "It's actually global health care in a flat world," we explained. "Going to another country for superior treatment at a much cheaper price than in the United States. For many who aren't insured or can't afford the spiraling costs of care in this country, it can be cheaper to fly halfway around the world to have certain procedures done."

"Honey," she replied, "my biggest problem is getting every doctor to use their fax machines for our record-keeping requests."

What's going on here? How is it that a key official in a country's health care system is struggling to bolster a technology that was outdated a decade ago, while an increasing number of patients completely bypass that system just to get affordable care?

Business is not keeping up with your needs, from the need to control your own life to the need for the best tools for the job. You have become a slave to infrastructure—what was supposed to help you now dictates too much of what you *can't* get done or, worse, the way you *have* to do things.

As we said at the outset, there is no malice here. Nobody's out to get you. But the system is holding you back and diminishing your contributions. Which is why hackers hack. And the gap is getting worse, which is why hacking is on a meteoric rise.

## THREE THINGS THAT ARE REALLY BROKEN

1. **Business just doesn't get it.** It's still far too corporate centered and is failing miserably at focusing on your needs.

2. **Your enablers control more than they enable.** Business's Trojan horse is to give you tools and procedures that force you to place limits on yourself. How you determine what's possible and what isn't is already built into most of your daily routines.

3. **Being an employee is a high-risk profession.** As an employee, there is absolutely no buffer between you and market forces. The current work contract between almost any employer and almost any employee is stacked completely in the company's favor.

## THREE THINGS THAT ARE REALLY BROKEN

Intuitively, you know this. You feel it in your bones every day. But what, exactly, is failing us? Here, we'll explore what's broken now, and in chapter 8 we'll look into what's coming up that will make hacking even more important.

## BIG BROKE 1:
## BUSINESS JUST DOESN'T GET IT

Business does not get the concept of being user centered. Despite decades of opportunities for change, almost everything we get handed to do our work is still corporate centered.

User-centered design works backward from your needs and goals. Typical examples you'd see as a consumer would be almost any high-end resort or hotel or some really great customer-focused online products like Gmail or Twitter. They feel good to use. You believe somebody was thinking of you when they were designed. Corporate-centered designs begin with the needs of the organization and attend to your needs only secondarily. Typical examples are almost any government procedure or form, customer service phone trees that last forever, most Microsoft products, and your most recent customer experience from hell.

Corporate-centered designs do serve an important purpose. There's nothing wrong with *sometimes* making everyone do things the same way. We wouldn't want air traffic controllers or nuclear plant operators or heart surgeons or the police or that cashier holding our credit card to just wing it whenever and however they feel like it. And every business does need some consistent processes to reduce costs and maintain quality. Some centralized controls are very necessary, and we'd experience horrific consequences if they did not exist.

The problem is in the mix. Almost 100% of workplace tools,

procedures, and reporting structures are still corporate centered—designed to fulfill the company's needs but not necessarily designed for your needs. Even after an explosion of empowering technologies that can be tailored just for you, business is still overwhelmingly focused on its needs and not enough on yours.

Wanna know how badly business doesn't get it? In 2007, the Economist Intelligence Unit, one of the world's foremost providers of global business analysis, found that CEOs believed the "most significant risk" to their global operations was human capital risk. That means that losing you or not equipping you to do your job properly was the one thing they believed would most jeopardize their results.

Let's compare that priority with what they actually did. What were the two risks that CEOs believed they managed most effectively? Financing risks and credit risks. (We all know how that turned out!) And what was among their worst managed risks? You got it: human capital. You.

So the two things CEOs thought they were managing superbly—finances and credit—are what spiraled out of control, endangering your livelihood. And the one thing they needed to do really well—equipping you to do your job—they know they've been managing poorly all along.

IBM searched for improvements in its *Global Human Capital Study 2008*. No surprises in what they found: The biggest organizational barrier was in human capital systems, the tools and processes designed to help you do your best. It turns out that everything from your workstation to your training and development to who's on your team and whom you report to is poorly integrated and varies in quality from great to horrible. Nothing works together in a cohesive manner to provide you with what you need to do your job.

This has been a critical, and critically underaddressed, problem for a long time. Two decades ago, the Jensen Group's ongoing study, *The Search for a Simpler Way*, found that the number one source of work complexity was lack of integration of all work systems, driven by a near total absence of user-centered design. Fast-forward to 2010: same result. Very little has changed.

For example, over sixty-five thousand *Simpler Way* study participants—20% senior execs, 45% midmanagers, and the remainder line workers—were asked the following:

- ▶ Which group consistently gets the *most* attention paid to simplifying things for them?
  - • 85% said: Senior executives.
- ▶ Which group consistently gets the *least* attention paid to simplifying things for them?
  - • 87% said: The workforce.

For two decades, we've looked at this problem from different angles, and the results are always the same: Corporate tools, structures, and procedures have remained the largest source of work complexity. Work systems have sucked for a long time, and they're not sucking any less.

Sure, there are a small number of amazing exceptions, like Zappos, where they offer you $2,000 to quit if you quickly discover that their culture isn't right for you, or Google, where you're paid to work on projects of your choosing 20% of the time. But most of us will never work at those companies, in those situations. If you're like most in the workforce, business has not made you or your work-level needs a priority.

This applies equally to big business, small business, nonprofits, and governments. The only difference is intent and empathy. Small businesses and nonprofits truly *want* to meet more of your work-level needs; they just are unlikely to ever have the required resources.

Because our needs are so often ignored, most of us take the easy way out and disengage. Employee engagement studies conducted by firms like Towers Watson, Gallup, and others show that, globally, fewer than one in five of us are fully engaged in and by our jobs. Try finding a champion chess player, mountain climber, or scientist who loathes his game. . . . Yet four-fifths of our workforce are loathing or just putting up with the game they're being paid to play.

Guess who makes up some of those who are fully engaged? Hackers hack in part because it keeps them loving what they do, or at least makes the crap manageable.

What business won't do for itself, you can do. You can change what sucks by hacking. The one passion that runs through the veins of every hacker is a ceaseless belief: There is always a better way!

## SUCKS-O-METER:
## EVALUATING YOUR COMPANY

**Scoring:** Pick a number between 0 and 5.

  **0: My company** really sucks at this.
  **5: My company** is fantastic at this.

1. My manager organizes and shares information in ways that help me work smarter and faster.
2. It's easy for me to find whoever or whatever I need to work smart enough, fast enough.
3. It's easy for me to get what I need to get my work done—right information, right way, in the right amount.
4. The tools, training, and procedures that the company requires me to use are easy to use and get me what I need as fast as I need it.
5. My time is respected, and my company is focused on using it wisely and effectively.

(continued)

## BIG BROKE 2:
## BUSINESS'S TROJAN HORSE

Your enablers are controlling you.

We knew from the outset that hacking redistributes power and control. The many ways business wields its control at work include mergers and restructuring; strategic plans and budgets; policies, procedures, and processes; and layoffs and edicts to "do more with less"—all designed to pass on market forces to you.

We set out to collect stories of how hackers bypass these forces. But something bigger emerged: business's Trojan horse, a more insidious form of control built into almost everything you do. In hacking lingo, a Trojan horse is a program that will take over control of your computer disguised as something benign—think of a virus embedded in a Sudoku game you downloaded.

We found that business builds this kind of beguiling but harmful Trojan horse into your everyday routines. It's using your own work tools and processes against you. The very things that are supposed to enable you are even better instruments of control.

The hacker who first called this to our attention was Gary Koelling. You met him in chapter 5; he's the director of emerging platforms at Best Buy.

His advice uncovers a Trojan attack you've probably experienced from your company: "Why bypass most corporate-supplied tools?" Gary asks. "So you can do your job the way it really needs to be done. The way we organize work matters. It informs who we are, who you are, how we relate, how you relate. Most of all, it affects what you believe you're capable of.

"From the beginning of the Industrial Revolution, when we gave up our cottage trades, we've relied on our employers to provide us with the tools we need to make a living and that, by extension, define our capabilities. Their tools, not ours. Their limits, not ours. It's pretty much been that way for the last hundred years. Still is. But that's changing. We're at an inflection point," Gary wisely observes.

"The tools we use to work and the tools we use to organize people are no longer exclusively owned or controlled by our employers. They're no longer prohibitively expensive or complicated. In fact, they're cheap, easy to use, and widely accessible. And nearly everyone under thirty-five years old has back-of-the-hand familiarity with them."

Workers everywhere are discovering just how poorly corporate tools and procedures serve their needs and are going outside their workplace to regain control over what they do.

Gary concludes, "Realizing that you have access to tools that are as good as or better than what your company provides fundamentally changes how you work. Everything from 'Who's my manager?' or 'What is a manager?' to 'What is work?' to 'Why work this way?' gets called into question. It's all up for grabs. You start to realize that there are too many corporate controls for you to succeed the way you need to."

That's business's Trojan horse: to give you tools and procedures that force you to place limits on yourself. How you determine what's possible and what isn't is built into most of your daily routines. "Well, of course I have to delete all emails after thirty days . . . and work with this team and not that one . . . and spend time on this and not that . . . and manage projects this way and not that way. . . . All that is programmed into my toolkit and our procedures."

The tools you use affect how you make decisions and how you get things done. Even a well-intentioned infrastructure can end up making you work harder, not smarter, if the way you need to work is different from what was built for you.

Again: This is not malicious. No company is out to get you . . . there is no hidden workplace conspiracy. But business's priority most definitely is herding you into predetermined paths that it believes will lead to the most predictable, profitable, and manageable outcomes for the firm. Its priority is also simplified control. Fewer variations in tools and processes mean less complexity and less work for the people above you.

The infrastructure you use to get your job done is becoming a more important tool of control than budgets, plans, hierarchy, or your boss. In ways that are hidden in plain sight, your tools and infrastructure have the power to either free you to imagine that anything is possible—and enable you to do whatever you can imagine— or deliberately confine you to someone else's predetermined path.

This helps us see great places to work in new ways: The infrastructure you use must value your time as much as it does the company's, it must make it easy for you to share your energy and ideas, and it must help you achieve almost anything that you can imagine, not just channel your efforts down predetermined paths. Does yours currently do that?

Hackers are the ones who believe every tool can and should accomplish all of this.

## WORK-AROUNDS FROM THE FIELD

**Bringing Science into the Twenty-first Century** from midmanager Matt: "I work at a large science museum. I care very deeply about my job, because I believe that being inspired by science and gaining an enthusiasm for learning is important for everyone. But I have to use some rather backward, unconventional, and often outright banned techniques to get my job done. For example:

"Even though we use multimedia as teaching tools, we are restricted from using YouTube at work. Recently I was asked to put together a fund-raising video. Rather than take five weeks to produce it with our own video production facilities, I did it overnight at home, posted it on YouTube, and sent the link to our list of alumni and donors. The response was bigger than anything previously done.

"We use unauthorized tools like Google Calendar for scheduling; Flickr for sending photos; wikis for collaboration; Gmail accounts for storing work emails to keep our puny in-boxes from overflowing.

"Our purchasing and accounting systems are equally locked down. Here my hack was soft—relationship based. I had lunch with the head of accounting and started a conversation that eventually led to purchasing complexities. She offered to wave a magic wand over my account to make my purchases a lot easier, with a winked warning: 'Keep in mind that you didn't know that this isn't the way it's done.'"

## BIG BROKE 3:
## BEING AN EMPLOYEE IS A HIGH-RISK PROFESSION

As an employee, you experience some of the highest exposures to risk and market forces in business, and no company is going to protect you—not anymore.

In 2009, after already imposing unpaid leave on everyone, British Airways asked its entire workforce of forty thousand to work for free for up to a month. Similar scenarios were played out all across the globe, in nearly every industry: "To keep your job, you're going to have to sacrifice even more than you already have."

There's no denying this reality. Headlines from the past couple of years: DOW HASN'T BEEN THIS BAD SINCE 1931 . . . THE NEW JOB-LESS: WHY IT'S DIFFERENT THIS TIME . . . WORST ECONOMIC CRISIS IN 70 YEARS . . . FOUNDATION OF NEW WORLD ORDER IS UNCERTAINTY.

Some cite 2009, with countless similar stories—FedEx slashing the pay of thirty-five thousand employees, Enterprise Rent-A-Car ending its fifty-one-year history of no layoffs, the terms of the bailout of Detroit—as the official death of "Our employees are our greatest asset." Actually, the death certificate was posted just before the economic collapse, on January 10, 2007. And a piece of it is probably in your closet.

That's the date Polartec LLC was created from the bankrupted assets of Malden Mills Industries, makers of that fleece in your closet. A decade earlier, in 1995, the Malden Mills factory burned down. CEO Aaron Feuerstein paid full salaries to all his employees for three months while it was rebuilt, even though there was no work, no products were being made, and no revenue was coming in. At the time, his actions were heralded as the gold standard in caring for one's employees. By 2001, Feuerstein lost control of his company to creditors, and most of the jobs he had protected were moved off-shore to China. By 2007, the company's underfunded pension plan was abandoned, leaving fifteen hundred employees with nothing but broken promises.

What took a decade for Malden Mills happened all at once for the rest of American businesses. The sea change of 2009, the worst of the crisis, was a new willingness to openly declare "Employees are our greatest asset" for what it was—a public relations myth.

Let's never again confuse a company's short-term needs with any kind of commitment: Employees may be the ones keeping the wheels on the bus, but they will *always* be thrown under it when the time comes. They will always be among the first assets to be sacrificed when a company faces threats. Almost every company that made it to 2010 did so by proving that its survival was far more important than anyone who worked for it.

And let's not blame this on the lousy economy or on those companies. All that the crisis did was to open our eyes to the myth and force us to accept reality.

Companies have the right and the obligation to fight for their survival. Leadership was just doing its job when it let you or your friend go. Even with small firms, where employees are treated like family, at the end of the day, they're not family. They, too, will be let go to save the company.

Accept it. There is zero security in being someone else's employee. Barring a drastic change in how capitalism works, in today's world only fools would tie their success to their company's success. (Unless they own it.)

Once upon a time, you chose to be someone's employee if you wanted more security than being an entrepreneur could offer. Your seniority, expertise, and leadership skills used to matter. Your loyalty used to matter. Your performance used to matter. None of that matters anymore. You could deliver superhuman results and be out the door tomorrow, with worthless stock options and no health benefits or pension even though they were "guaranteed" by the company. Now, as an employee, there is absolutely no buffer between you and market forces. And unlike an entrepreneur or majority shareholder, you have absolutely no say in how that plays out. You feel all the consequences but have no levers to pull to affect the outcome.

Being anyone's employee means you have the highest possible exposure to risk. Most companies are redesigning themselves to pass on any market volatility directly to you, without delay or hesitation. The current work contract between almost any employer and almost any employee is stacked completely in the company's favor.

As *Time* magazine noted in its September 2009 cover story, "Unemployed Nation": "America now faces the direst employment landscape since the Depression. It's troubling not simply for its sheer scale but also because the labor market, shaped by globalization and technology and financial meltdown, may be fundamentally different from anything we've seen before. . . . The jobs crisis offers us an opportunity to think in profound ways about how and why we work, about what makes employment satisfying, about the jobs [we all] can and should do best."[1]

Several months later, *BusinessWeek*'s cover story was entitled "The Disposable Worker." At the same time, *The Wall Street Journal* declared, GROWTH HITS 6-YEAR HIGH: EMPLOYERS REMAIN CAUTIOUS ABOUT HIRING. Enough said.

So what to do? We know that we can't wait for governments or business to do that profound new thinking. And when it comes to changing your own employment landscape, not everyone can be an entrepreneur, freelancer, or boss with a golden parachute. Lots of us need to remain employees. So until the employee/employer contract is changed (see chapter 10 for where to push for change and which companies are trying), being anyone's employee will remain high-risk.

If you're someone's employee, you have five options:

1. **Be lucky.** A select few companies have already begun to rewrite the contract. Find one and you're golden.
2. **Accept the risk.** Get the best job you can and pray.
3. **Change the risk by hacking.** Rework the contract by hacking what you can. Ensure that more tools and procedures meet your needs, not just the company's.

4. **Be a part-time entrepreneur.** Take a full-time job. Know that at some point you *will* be screwed, and prepare for that eventuality by having a small business on the side.

5. **Combine 3 and 4.**

If you must be someone's employee, and since being lucky isn't a reliable strategy, our advice is number five: Hack to ensure that you have what you need to succeed at your day job and so you have the time and energy to pursue your small-business dreams.

## TIME TO CHOOSE:
## WILL YOU BE THE BUG OR THE WINDSHIELD?

Business isn't user centered. . . . All your tools are actually Trojan horses focused on increasing controls. . . . Being anyone's employee means accepting the highest possible risk. . . . These dynamics are forcing everyone to make some kind of choice about controlling their own destiny. Clearly, the global economy and your company aren't worried about you or your best interest. Only you can watch out for you.

Is hacking the best choice for you, the best way to take back control? For many, it's becoming not only the best option, but the only one.

Within a few decades, business might fix these big brokes. In the meantime, you'll need to choose: Will you get squashed by these forces or will you do something to protect yourself and ensure the best possible outcome?

## WORK-AROUNDS FROM THE FIELD

**Unplugging to Work Anywhere, Anytime** from Nancy, whose company decided that wireless networks were too much of a security risk; despite this easy and cheap alternative, everyone had to plug in a cable whenever they wanted to get online. Nancy knew this was silly, so she bought a $20 wireless access point at Best Buy and set it up under her desk behind a filing cabinet. She distributed the password key to the folks she trusted. Suddenly, her enterprising and motivated teammates were able to do their work from anywhere in the office. In addition to increasing everyone's productivity, this hack gave them more time for life outside of work.

**Rig the Process for Innovation** from Erik: "I run eLearning for one of the world's largest pharmaceutical companies. eLearning is changing so fast, it's rare that the more established vendors will be able to deliver what we need. But corporate purchasing policies require me to go to them—at least at first. Yet doing so would be a big waste of time for all involved. So I write the RFP [request for proposal] in a way that pretty much guarantees that the approved vendors will bow out, opening the door for me to use the right ones for the job."

# 8

# WHAT'S AHEAD

There is nothing so useless as doing efficiently
that which should not be done at all.

—Peter Drucker, the ultimate management guru

## FOUR FORCES WHERE HACKERS WILL PLAY
## A KEY ROLE IN OUR FUTURE

Sometimes the powers that be need help seeing new possibilities.

Carlos is a very talented IT security guru. He helps clients prevent
systems breaches and penetrations. A while back, he was pitching
one of the biggest credit card processing centers because he knew
they were extremely vulnerable, and that wasn't fair to people like
you. (Their card is definitely one that's in your wallet.) "Senior management just didn't think they needed our services; they thought
they were perfectly safe with what they had," he recalled.

"So I went to the client's site, sat in their lobby with my laptop, and
logged in to their wireless network," Carlos continued. "Then, using
my company's security software, I pulled customers' real-time credit
card transactions off their production system and sent them to the

execs from their own email accounts along with a note telling them what I'd done and how easily I did it—all while sitting in their lobby. The CEO met with me immediately, and shortly after that we had a contract."

Because they're so attuned to flaws in infrastructures, as well as the unrealized and unlimited possibilities, hackers often see things that remain invisible to many others, including those in control.

In the previous chapter, we explored what's currently broken for all employees everywhere. Here, we'll look into what's coming up: four emerging trends, already visible to the hackers among us, that will change the face of work. Four forces where hacking is likely to play a major role in the ultimate outcome—and how that means new opportunities for you.

The future belongs to hackers.

## FOUR EMERGING FORCES WHERE HACKERS WILL INFLUENCE THE OUTCOMES

1. **Your Digital Footprint Takes Over.** Are you OK with how business will interpret every breath you take, every move you make? Hackers will be the ones proactively managing their measures, taking more control of how their own information gets used.
2. **Gen Y Hits a Tipping Point.** Today's leaders will not be able to stop an entire generation's focus on personal efficiency. Gen Y'ers will not share previous generations' ethical quandaries about hacking— if that's what's required for them to do great work, that's what will happen.

## FORCE 1:
## YOUR DIGITAL FOOTPRINT TAKES OVER

**What's changing?** Business's next battle for control over you will be aggressively capturing and monitoring your digital footprint.

**What will be different because of the change?** Thousands of data points, created by your every behavior and decision, will be collected and analyzed—whether you like it or not.

**Who gains, who loses?**[1] If you're not careful, employers will gain even more control over you. But hackers will use three core strategies to manage their own information and take back some control.

EVEN WITH THE BEST TECHNOLOGY and best intentions, anyone who tracks your data without really knowing you can misinterpret what they're seeing and really mess up your life. Learn from the worst-case scenario of Hasan Elahi.

3. **Co-creation Comes to Work.** Hackers know more than any executive about how to design *useful* corporate structures and tools. If companies ever get serious about *morebetterfastercheaper*, hacker employees will get to rework centralized designs, and leaders will become their willing students.

4. **Radical Transparency Grows Everywhere.** We can leverage new media in unprecedented ways. We can easily raise our voices in unity and push for changes in ways that were never possible before. Will you? Join the hackers who are already doing so.

Elahi is an art professor at Rutgers University whose life changed completely in June 2002. He was mistakenly whisked away from airport security, held at an INS detention facility, and questioned by the FBI. They suspected him of terrorist activities related to 9/11. After several months, he was eventually able to prove it was all a mix-up. His profile had been collected incorrectly and then completely misinterpreted. This process did irreparable damage to his career and personal life—all because of what was essentially a clerical error.

To ensure that never happened again, Elahi put his entire life online at TrackingTransience.net. He can prove where he is and what he's doing almost every minute of every day. He posts photos and screen captures of *every* part of his life online: what he eats, where he's been, bathrooms he uses, lists, receipts, everything!

Granted, it's unlikely that your workplace profile will ever cause those kinds of problems for you or make it necessary for you to react as Elahi did, but the career lesson to be learned is extremely important: Right now, a software vendor who doesn't know you or your situation is building a way to capture your digital footprint—your log-in times, your email habits, your social network, presentations you've made, what courses you've taken, and much more—so your boss can more aggressively manage you by your own numbers. And you will have no control over how that profile is used or what conclusions the software predisposes your boss to make.

You need to decide if you're OK with that, and if not, what you're going to do about it.

As Elahi explains, "If we do not take control of our own information, and define ourselves—other people will define us for us."

Completely new ways are emerging to manage you and define you by your numbers. Not just old-school ways, like how many hours you work or widgets you make or sell. But new, digitally precise measures that can be combined to provide your employer with completely new views of you.

Every breath you take, every move you make, every bond you break, every step you take: They'll be watching you. Including studying hundreds of data points:

- Your average response time to emails, voice mails, IMs, tweets—broken down by customers, co-workers, and superiors
- Your most productive days of the week and most productive times of each day
- Who's in your social network, which of them helped you the most last year, and which helped you the least
- Your BMI (body mass index . . . yes, even how much you weigh—any employee of grocery store chain Safeway with a BMI of 30 or more has to pay more for health care than other employees)

That which can be captured and analyzed can be used to control you—or at least maneuver you into behaving—and force you into working exactly the way they think you should work.

If you Google "analytics" or "performance management software" and dig into these topics, you will find that what we're describing isn't fully realized—*yet*. Software providers are still working through which methods are most efficient for collecting all that data, and business leaders are still working through how to use what they're collecting.

For example: A recent study by the Human Capital Institute found that about half the companies they surveyed still can't connect the performance data they already collect on you to the skills required for your job.

Still, the excruciatingly painful reality is that business must squeeze every ounce of productivity out of you that they can, and if they think that microexamining your digital records will help them do that, they will. In 2009, IBM interviewed over twenty-five hundred chief information officers for their study *The New Voice of the CIO*. When they asked CIOs to identify their most visionary plans, analytics and business intelligence was number one on the list, with relentless cost cutting driving all their activities. Being user centered (focused on your needs) wasn't even on the list.

What's ahead is supersized performance management.

What makes this something to be concerned about is not that business will eventually perfect this approach. They won't. (Remember, this is the gang who thought they were on top of financial and credit risks just months before the bottom fell out!) It's that you're the guinea pig who suffers while they try. Their holy grail is finding better numbers to manage you by, and you'll be subjected to all sorts of new directives and stupid-work that lock you into new tools and procedures while they fumble their way through each one.

Even if you work in a digitally Neanderthal environment, you're not safe. Every one of us is part of a work ecosystem. So this force will be used to track you through your connections to outside vendors, customers, even your competitors. One way or another, your company will record your digital footprint.

Think of your digital footprint at work like your credit score in your personal life. While someone else controls how it comes together and how it gets used, it's still *your* profile, and you have to actively manage what you can because it is used to make judgments about you.

Hackers use three core strategies to manage their own information and take back some control.

1. **Negotiating the Deal:** Most companies consciously hide how they build your digital footprint. To counter this, we've heard stories of savvy new hires who asked to know, up front, what portion of their performance management

assessment would be built digitally and from what sources. This puts them in a better position for the next two strategies. While this Soft Hack is still rare, the practice is likely to take off as the use of digital footprints grows.

2. **Upping the Positives:** Outside of work, you know how to rally your network and get them to post positive reviews online, right?

Do the same thing at work. If you know that one of your measures is how you use your social network, make sure people post how their connection to you made a difference in their work. If your response times are tracked, then make sure your most important customers and closest teammates comment on how responsive you are. That way, even if the data show that your average response times could be better, you've collected new data from those who are most important.

And don't passively hope that the company finds these things. Package them and send them to key managers prior to scheduled performance reviews. Or better yet, post them online, where they'll be sure to find them on their own.

Still, these are fairly mainstream hacks that leave you reacting to whatever the company wants to do. If your goal is to truly control more of your own destiny, here is the ultimate footprint hack. . . .

3. **Reduce the Size of Your Digital Footprint:** Think back to chapter 5 and why Gary Koelling advised you to build your own toolkit separate from whatever the company wants you to use: The more you can wean yourself from the company's infrastructure, the more you control how you get work done. That infrastructure also creates your footprint.

The more corporate-supplied tools and processes you use in your company, the bigger your digital footprint will be—which means you're generating lots of corporate-owned numbers that can be used to control you. The more you can use your *own* tools and the more you hack around company procedures, the *smaller* your digital footprint will be—which means greater control over your measures, your projects, your team, and your life.

Of course, you'll always be locked into some portion of their infrastructure, leaving some of your footprint forever within their control. A store manager at McDonald's, for example, can't go too far off the grid. Every burger and shake she makes and every breath she takes are tightly managed through that infrastructure.

But hack what you can. For example, if some of your critical communications flow through an outside server like Gmail instead of their SharePoint server, it will be a lot harder for your company to data-mine your communications or restrict the size of your inbox.

Mind you, there's still the imperative not to misuse (or lose!) critical corporate data. But from everything we've seen so far, you're better off using tools from Google or open source providers than some provider that HR got locked into five years ago. Regardless of how you accomplish it, managing your digital footprint is likely to be a critical dimension of who gets to define you and your work for years to come.

## FORCE 2:
## GEN Y HITS A TIPPING POINT

**What's changing?** Generation Y (folks born during the early 1980s or after) hits critical mass and becomes a workplace power to be reckoned with.

**What will be different because of the change?** For the first time since the dawn of the Industrial Revolution, the majority of the workforce will place as much emphasis on their personal productivity needs as on organizational needs. To accomplish this, they may choose to hack or they may not. But for this generation, hacking will no longer be an ethical dilemma: "It's just one of our options. If hacking is what we need to do, so be it."

**Who gains, who loses?** The companies that learn to embrace this shift in thinking will enjoy a major competitive advantage over those that don't. You want to work at a company that "gets" this. Avoid those that don't like the plague.

SUE HENNINGES is a senior learning and development consultant for MFS Investment Management, the firm that established the first mutual fund in the United States over eighty-five years ago. And she has realized that she needs to start thinking younger. That's because she asked her team to consider the impact of Gen Y and how their hacking work will change their workplace. Here's how Sue ended up agreeing with the views of Bijan Zandbod, a co-op student from Northeastern University:

Sue, the Boomer: "Older workers misinterpret Gen Y's insistence on personal efficiency as disrespectful. These kids have a very short window in which to prove themselves. They don't have weeks or months to wait for the company to remove barriers or get them what they need. My biggest takeaways from our conversations are: Flexibility matters, tailoring to each person's needs matters. A lot more of all work processes needs to be more negotiable, more adaptable. But in the end, results still matter."

Bijan, the Gen Y'er: "My reaction to hacking work is that it's just efficiency, personal efficiency. It's not about our confidence or attitude so much as it is [that] we just need to learn and do as much as possible as quickly as possible. We don't worship CEOs or any leader. We don't see them as someone who can withhold access or set rules that bar us from participation. Instead, we see them as a future me. That's why we see them as approachable and why we do approach them . . . to learn as much as we can as quickly as we can, but especially to change whatever doesn't work. To be efficient.

"My biggest takeaways," Bijan concludes, "are that today's leaders are not going to be able to stop an entire generation's focus on what drives us. Personal efficiency is how we define and find our self-worth. We instantly know when something is worthwhile or isn't . . . when it is or is not worth our time or effort. And a lot of what's happening right now in most companies just isn't working."

Our research, part of which was a hack itself, reveals two Gen Y truths hidden in plain sight. Sue's and Bijan's conversations were one set of over 350 that we sponsored around the world during 2008–2009 to better understand Gen Y's impact on the world of work, relating specifically to benevolent hacks.

Building upon the work of others, such as Don Tapscott's book *Grown Up Digital*, we wanted to explore hacking as a Gen Y phenomenon. It's a given that this is a generation of digital natives: Pew Research Center's 2010 Pew Internet & American Life Project found that 93% of teens from twelve to seventeen are online regularly. Nowadays, even some of the yellow buses that take these kids to school have built-in Wi-Fi routers, and teachers are leveraging wikis and smartphones and anything else they have access to in order to meet their students' learning styles. The unknown was: Would they go beyond heavy use of the systems they are handed, and would they actively take control of those systems?

Our hypothesis was that this would be a generation of hackers—that the first generation to be raised within a total democratization of information would certainly rework anything and everything that got in their way.

We were partly spot-on and also way off.

We began with a hack of our own, writing a computer script to pull email addresses from university and job site databases, yielding over 350,000 potential participants. That netted us over 800

Gen Y interviewees with about an hour's worth of work. (Yep, that's hacking. Personal productivity at its finest.) We then paired those Gen Y'ers with Boomer and Gen X managers we already had in our database. In all, we sponsored over 350 conversations among Boomers, X'ers, and Y'ers, ranging from just two people chatting online to entire staff retreats dedicated to digging deep into the impact of Gen Y and hacking in the workplace.

You'll find some of those conversations and more at HackingWork .com, but here are the top two findings:

1. **Gen Y will definitely hack their work, whenever and however it suits them—and only then.** Bijan's conclusion matches what we found almost everywhere—Gen Y will hack around almost anything that gets in the way of their personal productivity. Or how they define productivity: If they need to work around a process so they don't have to work weekends and nights the way their Boomer parents did, they'll do it without thinking twice.

   The impact of Gen Y hacking their workplace cannot be overstated. They're better equipped than any previous generation with the tools and skills to work around almost anything that gets in their way, and more important, they do not see work-arounds as an ethical issue. If hacking is what's necessary to be productive, well, that's not their problem, that's a problem that the institution or their boss created. Add that to what they saw their parents go through—learning the hard way that corporate loyalty carries no rewards—and it's easy to understand why Gen Y'ers see benevolent hacking as a practical approach to problems in their working lives.

   However, we were way off on our assumptions that all of Gen Y would be revolutionary with their hacks—that they'd create rapid change, on a massive scale, all on their own.

When we looked across responses, we found a normal bell curve distribution of attitudes: Some will be revolutionary in how they focus on their needs and their team's needs; others will be more evolutionary and willing to go along with whatever the organization's needs are. Most will be somewhere in between.

Our findings matched a 2009 MTV study about Gen Y's attitudes toward happiness: "Youth will take a very active role in creating their own happiness. . . . [But they] will be indifferent about things they state make them unhappy—choosing not to take action to solve larger problems that don't affect them directly. . . . It's not about apathy, but more a sense of being practical about what they feel they have influence over and not wasting time on areas where they feel they cannot make a difference."[2]

Throw in economic turmoil and Gen Y is likely to appear schizo. In 2009, nearly 37% of Spain's Gen Y'ers couldn't find work. In France it was 24% and around 18% in the United States and Great Britain.[3] They are already being called "the Lost Generation," as the job crisis has hit young people especially hard. Some in this generation will act like their parents and play by the rules just to keep whatever job they can get, while many will see hacking and fixing their poorly designed work tools and processes as the only way to ensure their own success once they are employed.

So don't look for predictability on where, when, how, and why Gen Y will hack. If a form that they filled in last week suddenly bothers them this week, they'll hack it. If they feel they can hack one systemwide process but not another, they'll work passionately to hack that one process while being compliant participants in the other.

To an outsider, these behaviors may not make sense or have a pattern. To Gen Y, the pattern is whatever's practical at that moment under those circumstances. They'll hack whatever and whenever they feel they can make a difference, and they'll follow other corporate-centered processes where it makes the most sense to do so—for them, from their perspective.

What this means to you: If you're a Millennial, feel free to be fickle and inconsistent (at least in how others see you)—as long as you're producing results! If you're older, work hard to see root causes—what's causing Gen Y'ers to hack one area and not another. You'll then have a rare window into new ways to quickly improve employee productivity.

2. **There is major tension among the generations, and it's not coming from Gen Y.** A sampling from the conversations we sponsored: "This generation has a sense of entitlement. They look for higher starting salaries, flexible work schedules, and company-provided BlackBerrys." . . . "They want constant feedback. Instant performance reviews!" . . . "Gen Y believes that data acquisition and ripping is thinking." . . . "The whining has got to stop. I've actually heard things from these kids like 'I need to bring my dog to work on Tuesdays' and 'I don't like the color of my office.' Enough already."

We found large amounts of tension, biases, and generational rifts running through most of the conversations we sponsored. There is still an intense difference among the generations. But little of it was driven by Gen Y. Overall, Boomers and X'ers appear to have many negative attitudes and beliefs about Gen Y—mostly about the younger generation's sense of entitlement.

Our findings mirror a 2009 study by the Pew Research Center that found almost eight in ten people believe there is a major difference in the points of view of younger people and older people today—the highest spread since 1969, when conflict over the war in Vietnam and civil and women's rights was at its peak. When asked to identify where older and younger people differ most, 47% said social values and morality.

This is why the ethos of benevolent hacking, discussed in chapter 6, and finding ways to work together, covered in chapter 11, are so important. Gen Y's focus on personal productivity could intensify divisions within the workplace if we're not all trying to find common ground. As the majority of the workforce shifts from Boomers to Gen Y (both are larger populations than the one in the middle, Gen X), having the two hating and working against each other could spell disaster for most companies.

## THE TIPPING POINT

When will Gen Y hit critical mass and become a power to be reckoned with?

To uncover this, the Jensen Group turned to alliance partners e3 Unlimited, a London-based talent management firm, and the European School of Management. Here are some of their findings.

**WHEN WILL GEN Y's TIPPING POINT HIT YOU?**

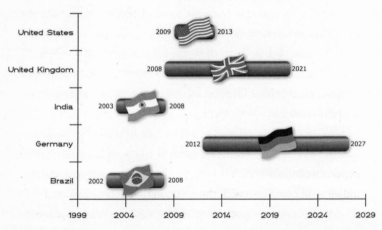

**India and Brazil Are Already Feeling It:** Each country's demographics create a unique Gen Y tipping point for that country. Here is a sampling of five. **The left side** of each country's bar is when Gen Y numbers become significant—they outnumber Boomers. **The right side** of the bar is when Gen Y'ers become the largest segment of the country's entire population.

**2011–2014: Global Gen Y Tipping Point Begins.** There are so many factors—country demographics, percentage of employment within each industry, and so on—that an exact date for a global tipping point is impossible to accurately predict. Some niches, industries, and locations are already long past the tipping point, while others still have a few years before the storm hits.

But as a lens through which to view Gen Y's overall impact on the New World of Work, look for a significant shift during the three-year window of 2011–2014. Depending on where you live and what you do, you will likely witness a surge in Gen Y influence. And it will continue to grow after that.

That means leaders have no time to waste to figure out how to address Gen Y's hacking capabilities. And we all should expect a lot more hacking to occur in the very near future, in every aspect of work.

SIDETRIP

## CREATIVE DESTRUCTION COMES TO WORK

**Two men** long gone, one known for attempts to free the proletariat, the other known for free market forces, are driving the future of hacking.

Aside from the political baggage he piled onto it, Karl Marx had one idea that was about 160 years ahead of its time. The German philosopher, economist, and father of Marxism argued that the workforce actually owned the means of production. Wishful thinking. Industrial age views would still reign for a few centuries. But now that we've moved into a knowledge and service economy (which is highly linked to the efforts of each individual), combined with the empowering technologies of the last decade, the workforce actually does control more and more means of production.

*(continued)*

Capitalists are not big on Marx, but they love Joseph Schumpeter. During the first half of the twentieth century, Schumpeter, an economist and political scientist born in Austria, popularized the idea of "creative destruction" in economics. In his vision, entrepreneurs force changes in the marketplace by creating new products and industries that wreak havoc on or wipe out old ones. Modern-day examples are how Walmart changes retailing wherever it plops its stores and how iPods and iPhones have changed the music and smartphone industries. Schumpeter's ideas are cited anytime businesses exert change on *external* markets.

Think of what's happening now as these two guys come together in the afterlife—hackers have married their visions. The power of Marx's proletariat to organize work, people, and ideas is now equal to, and sometimes better than, that of their employers. And by hacking, they're bringing Schumpeter's creative destruction *inside* companies, whether their bosses want it or not.

## FORCE 3:
## THE AGE OF CO-CREATION COMES TO WORK

**What's changing?** Employers are going to have to trust their employees a lot more. Trust them to change, tweak, modify, and push back on processes, tools, and procedures that are currently protected by senior management.

**What will be different because of the change?** Faster, cheaper, better results. More engagement, participation, and innovation. And significantly less ego—senior management will have to learn to let go of more than they're currently willing to. A lot more.

**Who gains, who loses?** To the agile and those willing to adapt go the spoils. For those, expect higher employee retention, motivation, and satisfaction, as well as a greater ability to drive bottom-line results.

"FOR A COUPLE HUNDRED YEARS... the only ones who could write doctrine were the select few," Colonel Charles Burnett, director of the U.S. Army's Battle Command Knowledge System, told *The New York Times*. "Now, imagine the challenge in accepting that anybody can go on the wiki and make a change—that is a big challenge, culturally."

You think your senior team has difficulty letting go? Imagine what it must be like for those on top of the ultimate command-and-control structure! And yet they are. To the army, field manuals are the ultimate bibles. They give instructions on all aspects of army life. In July 2009, the U.S. Army began a pilot program where anyone with an ID—from privates to generals—can log on and rewrite field manuals chosen for the program.

The army's leadership has the same fear of loss of control that your senior execs have. Not all the brass are on board. Yet the changes are being made. For example, a staff sergeant in Iraq made changes to the Stryker Brigade's field manual so that infantry soldiers would better understand their role in collecting intelligence.

Some controls are still in place. Of the army's more than five hundred field manuals, fifty or so are "capstone" guides that are not open to co-creation—like those on interrogation or counterterrorism and those with specialized guidance, like how to stay warm during cold-weather operations. Still, the goal, say the officers behind the effort, is to do a much better job of tapping into the experience of battle-tested soldiers rather than relying on those who are too far removed from the action to write these field bibles.

If an organization whose job descriptions include the most life-threatening situations imaginable is turning to co-creation and crowdsourcing, any company can.

**Seeing structure and tools through the lens of co-creation.** Few would debate the need for a top-down, somebody's-gotta-make-decisions-for-you approach when it comes to developing new medicines, right? Certainly none of us patients could ever know enough to change the process of how meds are researched, developed, tested, and prescribed, right? No one would be foolish enough to try to hack such an important process—lives are at stake!

Yet they are. Members of PatientsLikeMe.com are changing the process of how drugs are developed for diseases like ALS and HIV/AIDS. Far more than a support community, these patients are hacking into the process of how drugs are made and influencing what pharmaceutical companies deliver back to them.

By sharing their complete medical histories and treatments in minute detail, they're bypassing the double-blind process set up by drug manufacturers and government agencies. Results include reporting drug side effects directly to regulators without waiting for the manufacturers to do so on their time frame and without any of the drug makers' spin on what they're experiencing.

As a result, better drugs are in the pipeline faster and with more insight into who will best benefit from them. Ultimately, this means more sales for the drug companies that co-create most fully and better medications for the people who need them.

Most important, they did so without permission and without being invited to participate—at least initially. Even with all the inherent concerns about information privacy and the need to ensure scientific rigor and efficacy, drug companies are beginning to see the light. "Patients will keep pressuring all of us in the direction of more openness," says Trevor Mundel, head of development for drug maker Novartis. Mundel reports that one drug trial was greatly accelerated by partnering with these patient hackers. Says health care consultant Matthew Holt, "The cat's out of the bag. This is happening and the world has to deal with it."[4]

Must deal with it indeed.

The debate is over. It's no longer a question of *whether* business leaders will cede control and power over their structures and tools and truly partner with those who use those structures. The only remaining questions are "When?" "How?" and "To what end—how do we create the most value for all concerned?"

**Business trusts vendors and customers more than its own employees.** Co-creation is not a new idea. C. K. Prahalad— management consultant, business author, and, until his death in 2010, a professor of corporate strategy at the University of Michigan's School of Business—called co-creation "the next practice in value creation" in his 2004 book *The Future of Competition.*

Said Prahalad, "Co-creation . . . fundamentally challenges . . . the basic tenet of traditional economic theory: that the firm and the consumers are separate, with distinct, predetermined roles, and, consequently, that supply and demand are [separate] processes."[5]

Most big businesses have already rebuilt their supply chains in this manner. Co-creation allows vendors like dairy cooperatives and electronics manufacturers to choose the most efficient ways to restock the shelves of your favorite grocery store or discounter. The same is happening with customers: Super Bowl ads, Legos, Procter & Gamble products, the Danish beer Vores Øl ("Our Beer"), and CNN iReports have all been co-created by customers.

The U.K. supermarket division of Walmart, Asda, recently announced that its loyal customers will have a say in how the stores are run. "My ambition," said Asda CEO Andy Bond, "is to . . . enable our customers to help make decisions that have an impact on what we sell and how we sell it."[6]

So why isn't this happening a lot more *within* the workplace?

A recent study by the IBM Institute for Business Value found that companies that practice customer co-creation experience reduced costs, increased revenues, improved customer intimacy, and enhanced product innovation and differentiation. Later, in their study *The New Voice of the CIO*, IBM found that 87% of high-growth CIOs would be seeking customers' active participation on how to build their infrastructure. One CIO said the priority was to "change from a 'push' model to a 'pull' model, where the customer expresses requirements and IT responds immediately."[7] But there was no mention of you co-creating, influencing, or driving your infrastructure. Nor was there any mention of IT stopping its approach of pushing everything onto you, no mention of you having a say in requirements and IT rushing to respond.

Employers, wake up. It's time to trust your employees as much as you trust customers and vendors. Who knows better than they about what their job really requires? It's time to fundamentally challenge the basic tenet of *workplace* economic theory.

Prahalad issued his own post–economic crisis warning in 2009: "Now what [we] need is a system for addressing volatility. . . . More important [than just operational efficiency] are the abilities to scale up and down and reconfigure resources rapidly."[8] That's exactly what hackers offer: continuous adaptability.

It's no longer appropriate to insist that the firm's processes and structures must be predetermined and protected by senior management—that the design and the use and the control of corporate structures are somehow separate processes. They never were, and they certainly aren't now. Instead of locking rusty chastity belts around corporate procedures, reward employees for how their ongoing changes and improvements increase bottom-line results.

**A great example of co-creation . . .** Finnish mobile phone company Nokia is an unquestioned leader in the smartphone market, with 38% of the global handset market, twice as much as number two Samsung. But between the bad economy and competitors like Apple, RIM, Motorola, and Palm, that lead has been dropping steadily.

One of their solutions: Leverage social media and encourage critiques of the company by its own employees—inviting push-back that most firms would have shut down. Nokia set up online environments called BlogHub and Sphere specifically to encourage and capture employee rants on what they think needs changing—from its purchasing practices to how its software works.

More than an electronic suggestion box, these push-backs and critiques flow right into company R&D, which includes nearly one out of every three Nokia employees, or thirty-nine thousand people. Rapid changes in its touch screens, keyboards, and specialized local services for customers all have their origins in employee rants.

The key to all this? Senior management being "as open as you can be. Don't fear the social media space—embrace it. Accept and acknowledge criticism where it is fair. Don't just listen to feedback and comment—act on it," says Molly Schonthal, who heads social media for Nokia North America.[9]

**. . . And why that example still sucks.** The problem with Nokia's example is what's causing hackers everywhere to hack. It hinges on senior management being willing to embrace bottom-up co-creation by its employees. And so far, leadership's track record on this front has been less than stellar.

Let's be honest: Nokia is the exception, not the rule. (Why else would *BusinessWeek* herald their use of social media as a breakthrough innovation in an article entitled "Bring On the Employee Rants"? Encouraging, sponsoring, and incorporating procedural innovations from the bottom up is still news.)

And let's not glorify the exceptions too much. Nokia's leadership embraced employee rants only when they *had* to. Just like most companies out there.

Starbucks's CEO Howard Schultz loves telling a story about milk. As part of his efforts to ensure the quality of the millions of lattes and cappuccinos Starbucks serves, he forbade what had become the common practice of resteaming milk. That meant baristas were pouring millions of dollars of leftover milk down the drain. Now that economic pressures were hitting hard, somebody at corporate finally embraced a store manager's hacked solution: Put etched lines in the steaming pitchers so that the baristas would know how much milk to use for each size of a specific drink. Before, they just guessed.

Well, duh.

This is the root of business's problem. *First*, they try centralized, top-down solutions. *Eventually*, they wake up and tap into the wisdom within their organization, and then only when they *have* to.

And here's the worst part: As soon as things start working again, it's back to top-down, centralized control, meaning that daily innovations and useful changes in tools and processes happen only when the shit hits the fan again—which is the worst time to produce thoughtful, scalable, valuable solutions.

Hackers know more than any executive about how to design *useful* corporate structures and tools. Whenever companies get serious about *morebetterfastercheaper*, hacker employees will get rework power over centralized designs, and leaders will become their willing students.

Whenever business finally embraces the age of co-creation, the hackers among us will be our best advisers.

## FORCE 4:
## RADICAL TRANSPARENCY GROWS EVERYWHERE

**What's changing?** We're living through the largest increase in expressive capability in human history.

**What will be different because of the change?** Even command-and-control structures have now been democratized. No one's voice can be blocked. Everyone's views on their tools and work structures will be heard. That impacts all decisions about all work designs.

**Who gains, who loses?** If you're stuck in a traditional nontransparent company, hacking will get you unstuck. But ideally, seek out only those companies that really understand the value of transparency and deep employee engagement.

IT WAS JUST DAYS BEFORE IRANIAN PROTESTERS would take to the streets in June 2009. Just before they would tweet and post on Facebook and YouTube that which the Iranian government did not want the world to see. Some of it horrified us all.

Nine days before the disputed election in Iran, Clay Shirky, author of *Here Comes Everybody*, adjunct professor at New York University, and a prescient voice on the Internet's effects on society, spoke at the U.S. State Department—the same government agency that would soon ask Twitter to postpone a planned upgrade so that Iranian citizens could tweet their experiences to the world.

Shirky: "These tools don't get . . . interesting until they get technologically boring. It isn't when the shiny new tools show up that their uses start permeating society, it's when everybody can start taking them for granted. Now that media is increasingly social, innovation can happen anywhere. . . . We're starting to see a media landscape in which innovation is happening everywhere and moving from one spot to another. That is a huge transformation. The moment we're living through is the largest increase in expressive capability in human history."

Shirky then closed with critical advice to all who would listen: "The audience can talk back, but that's not the really crazy change. The really crazy change is the fact that they [your audience] are no longer disconnected from each other . . . [they] can talk directly to each other. The choice we face now is how can we make best use of this media even though it means changing the way we've always done it."[10]

To give you an idea about how far we have yet to go to live up to Shirky's advice: While Iranians were free to tweet from the streets during the 2009 crisis, aides to key decision makers in Washington, D.C., had to run out to their parking lots to view those tweets on their mobile phones because access to Twitter was restricted within their buildings and on their computers.

**Business has yet to learn some very critical lessons.** A decade before Shirky stood before the State Department, four gadfly authors took business to task in *The Cluetrain Manifesto*: "Markets are conversations. Through the Internet, people are discovering and inventing new ways to share relevant knowledge with blinding speed. As a direct result, markets are getting smarter—and getting smarter faster than most companies."[11]

That's a transformational idea that the entire wired population has adopted with a vengeance. (For quick tours of how everyone everywhere has jumped all over this, check out the videos "Did You Know 4.0" by xplanevisualthinking on YouTube and "Web 3.0" by Kate Ray on Vimeo.) Everyone gets this—except corporate leaders, that is.

### Among the game-changing lessons yet to be learned:

1. Business has lost control of the conversation with their employees—and *still* hasn't admitted that or dealt with the shift in control.

2. Everything gets done through conversations. No plan gets implemented, no tool gets used, and no procedure gets followed without conversations. Since business no longer controls those conversations, the workforce is now an equal partner. And it's *still* not being treated that way.

3. Since nobody's listening to their user-centered needs, employees are forced to turn away from the conversation and start hacking.

4. There is no hiding anything anymore. If it's important to those who are affected, anything that institutions try to keep behind closed doors will be shared openly and voraciously. This includes work-arounds. As they hack whatever senior management tries to control, employees will increasingly go public with what they're doing and what they know.

This is what happened in Iran. Protesters hacked around government-approved procedures for airing grievances and shared it all with the world. This is what happened in Sichuan, China, in 2008, when a massive earthquake hit the region. Using Twitter, Facebook, and YouTube, Chinese citizens worked around official media channels and exposed to the world that much of the devastation was caused by

HACKING WORK

officials who took bribes that resulted in the building of substandard structures, which increased the death tolls.

**And this is what's happening in business today: radical transparency.** During our research, we found a number of benevolent hackers who secretly got their bosses to listen to them through YouTube posts—mostly by creating a forum for customer outcries related to their projects and concerns. This practice will surely grow exponentially—at the same rate as the growth of Web tools and apps—as long as bosses continue not listening to their employees.

We found that immediately after the announcement of a restrictive corporate policy or procedure, employees were tweeting one another—at first complaining, then building solidarity, then sharing work-arounds . . . *within minutes* . . . often during the meetings while the policy was being announced! As information-moving tools grow simpler to use and more ubiquitous among the general population, this practice will surely skyrocket.

It is important, however, to put this in perspective. Radical transparency will not overthrow leaders or alter business's approach overnight. As with our findings relating to Gen Y, the workforce will likely follow a bell curve approach to radical transparency: some pockets of rapid-fire revolutionary actions, with the largest number of changes bubbling up over time. But even if the hacks take a while to hit critical mass, the conversation has already been radically altered. Business leaders should be prepared for a lot more push-back from the rank and file than they've ever seen before.

**We have seen the future, and you can, too.** Go to twitter.com/ zappos or blogs.zappos.com. Zappos is an online retailer that began like Amazon, focused on one product line—shoes—and surpassed $1 billion in gross merchandise sales after a decade of building a reputation for amazing customer service. Its Web site proclaims, "Customer service is everything. In fact, it's the entire company." Zappos must be doing something right: It was named number fifteen in *Fortune* magazine's 2010 "100 Best Companies to Work For";

one year earlier, Amazon had made it its biggest acquisition ever, purchasing Zappos for $1.2 billion on the day of closing.

We spoke with the CEO of Zappos, Tony Hsieh, who was one of the first major executives to embrace Twitter as a tool to promote radical transparency throughout a company. Hsieh posts tweets regularly and encourages all employees to do the same.

Those posts range from the routine ("What SKU are you talking about and I will look into it for you") to the ridiculous ("I wonder how many #aea09 attendees smell of orange gingery goodness") to the sublime ("Pondering life's big questions: What does Luke Skywalker do on Father's Day?") to a CEO sharing his daily musings ("At airport headed to our warehouse in KY. I get stage fright in front of so many shoes. I will just imagine them without clothes").

Tony Hsieh: "What you're calling radical transparency is just our culture. Everything is about the customer, and every conversation is out in the open. This reinvents a lot of decision making. [For example,] everyone who's hired into our Las Vegas office goes through four weeks of training, no matter what their position is. If you're an accountant or lawyer, you go through the same training that our customer loyalty reps [call center reps] go through—including learning about our company history, the importance of company culture and customer service, and two weeks of taking calls from customers.

"But more than just increasing everyone's participation during training," says Hsieh, "we upended the decision-making process so it considers the decisions that every trainee needs to make. At the end of the first week of training, we offer everyone in the class $2,000 to quit. This is a standing offer until the end of the fourth week. This may seem counterintuitive, but it weeds out people who are at Zappos just for a paycheck. We wind up with employees who are truly passionate about customer service and the company culture. This is because we honor the fact that every new hire needs to quickly decide, 'Is this the right place for me?' and not the other way around.

"By focusing on everyone's needs up front, we eliminate the need for a lot of hacking," concludes Hsieh. "That feeds right into our bottom line. The number one driver of our growth is that 75% of our orders are from repeat business. And our customers constantly tell us that a big reason they keep coming back is our culture of focusing on them—which happens through our employees."

As Hsieh says, radical transparency eliminates a lot of the need to go underground with hacks. Instead, most hackers' ideas flow easily through normal channels. So in the coming years, you are likely to find more underground hackers within traditional companies and less need to hack in more open cultures. In those more open firms, hacking will simply be called innovation.

## REDUX:
## WILL YOU BE THE BUG OR THE WINDSHIELD?

As in chapter 7, we'll close with a choice.

Beware your digital footprint. . . . Gen Y hits a tipping point. . . . Co-creation comes to work, along with radical transparency. . . .

These emerging trends are hitting workplaces now, and their impact will ramp up throughout the next decade. Each one forces new decisions on each of us: How will you take control of your own information? As more and more co-workers push for personal efficiencies, will you join in? If your management continues to protect its tools and procedures while your friend's company allows her to change, tweak, modify, and push back on hers, will you happily stay at your company? And will you leverage changing technologies and your social capital to push for changes?

As these trends unfold, you will have to choose: Will you get squashed by these forces or, like all hackers, will you do something to play a role in the outcome?

# WORK-AROUNDS FROM THE FIELD

**Oh, the Stories I Could Tell . . .** from Michael: "I'm a high-priced, high-end contract IT worker. Some of what I've seen in the past year: Lots of employees who work for the Evil Empire in Redmond are secretly forwarding all their email through Google's Gmail; they know that their own email product is too limiting and is extremely restrictive. Teams that installed webcams on their floor so they could tell where the boss was at all times; lots of people building SSH tunnels through the firewall so they can work from home, or proxies to surf sites that are totally blocked by the corporate firewall."

**Mirroring a Secured Network to Work from Home** from Seth: "Most companies focus on securing their networks from outside threats—they usually don't get around to full security within their firewall. They also don't provide the services their employees need, like giving us access to our work data from home. So I help my buddies by setting up rogue services inside the internal network. I set up a Web service, Dropbox, that acts like a file server that we can access from the Internet, so everyone gets secured access to their data both on their work PC and at home. We use port 443, which can't be blocked. Everything gets mirrored between work and home. [For how-tos, Google "proxy filtering" or "tunneling through the firewall."]

"What's critical to all this is our code of ethics—we police each other so there are zero security breaches, and we have a strong culture of ethics. This is about us being able to work the way we need to work, and hacking work-arounds only because our employer won't cooperate. They are far more concerned with their ROI and cutting costs than with how much extra work and inefficiency that creates for us."

# THE ELEPHANT
# IN THE ROOM

Named must your fear be before banish it
you can.

—Jedi master Yoda

## HOW PLAYING BY THE RULES HAS CHANGED

All right, all right, you get it: Hacking is the wave of the future. So
why are you still just sitting there?

Fear.

That's the elephant in the room. Let's address what should not be
ignored—FUD. (Fear, uncertainty, and doubt: a competitive strategy
coined in the 1970s by the IBM sales force. "Are you willing to risk
your job by picking those other guys? No one ever got fired for buying
IBM computers.")

Like almost anything in life, there's a spectrum of risk associated
with hacking. Risk carries both upsides (innovation, growth, competitive advantages, new opportunities) and downsides (the possibility of loss, being judged, and more). Let's explore all that and how
playing by the rules has changed.

We wrote this book for all potential hackers—essentially everyone who works. We figured everybody would want to learn about practices that would help them be more efficient and more effective. But as we ran drafts of the manuscript past hundreds of early readers, we quickly learned that hacking work is an emotionally charged topic. On their own, readers picked sides—"us" and "them." Many who built or obediently used company structures saw work-arounds as personal attacks: "Hacking is wrong." The other side felt, "At last . . . a way out!"

We discovered that these divisions are so deep that we couldn't ignore them or downplay their significance. You likely fall into one of two categories: those who hack and those who don't out of fear or the need to maintain the status quo.

## FEAR AND THE NEW HIERARCHY OF NEEDS

If you see yourself as a non-hacker, the biggest elephant in the room is likely to be "But I can't take the chance that my hacks might tick off the people who can fire me. Especially not during a tough economy."

Why would you give bosses that much power over your future when the only powers that truly matter reside within you and outside of your company? Why would you believe that the best you can hope for is fear-based survival? We need to get past that.

One cautious non-hacker gave us the key. She said, "Think about Maslow's hierarchy of needs. It seems like you're talking about the needs close to the top of his hierarchy, like self-actualization. Lower-level, everyday needs like food, shelter, and having a job have to be met before the higher-level ones can be pursued. Why should people who are worried about their paychecks hack their work? Why should the people who sign those paychecks be concerned about meeting their employees' higher needs when they should feel lucky to have a job?"

Because Maslow's hierarchy has been updated for the second millennium, that's why.

**Maslow's New Base-Level Needs:** If they didn't know it before, business leaders could have gotten the update from Thomas Friedman's *The World Is Flat*: Be prepared to compete with everyone, everywhere, for everything. Every company and everyone inside that company are instantly replaceable. And if you didn't know it before, the change has been force-fed to you during the past few years. Your essential base-level needs now are **food, shelter, a job,** *and* **your ability to compete for your own job every day.**

No matter what you do or where you do it, a change anywhere in the world at any time can suddenly pull your job out from under you.

Your ability to please your customers or your boss or your company is no longer key. Your only hope lies in your ability to adapt and continuously do better than you did yesterday no matter what is thrown at you.

Friedman called this ability "uploading." He focused specifically on using the latest tools and technologies to rapidly learn, borrow, create, or adapt so you can compete with anyone in the world for your own job, "rather than downloading them from commercial enterprises or traditional hierarchies."

That's why hacking is no self-actualizing luxury. Given business's current approach—corporate centered, not you centered—hacking is as necessary to your work as food and shelter are to your life. Business has proven that its priority is its own survival, not yours. Everything that deserves to be hacked—bosses who herd you into top-down approaches that are inefficient for you and your team; outdated and corporate-centered technologies that make your work harder; restrictive procedures and strict processes—is designed to ensure corporate survival and success. Unfortunately, most of what you're forced into *also* destroys your ability to upload and adapt at the rate you need to, destroying your ability to survive.

If you're worried about next week's paycheck, start hacking.

## GOOD FEAR, BAD FEAR

According to Buddhists, there is healthy fear and unhealthy fear. Healthy fear involves taking constructive steps to avoid a destructive outcome—like stopping smoking when you know what's going to happen if you don't. Unhealthy fear is being afraid of something that can't actually harm you or something you can do nothing about—think spiders or being struck by lightning.

Fear of negative consequences from hacking: good fear or bad?

Let us put this as plainly as we can: **Fear of hacking your work is an unhealthy fear.**

Here's what we can report to you: **Benevolent hackers do not get fired.** And the best get promoted!

After tapping into this underground army, we sat down with leaders, managers, and frontline workers and asked, "What do you think?" Since this was the first time that hacking work has been outed, we wanted to know how the masses might react.

These non-hackers fell into three distinct groups. The pro minority pumped their fists in the air, crying, "Yes! It's about time!" The con minority were in denial: "No way. . . . Hacking doesn't happen that much." What fascinated us most was the third group—the majority. They were cautious and timid: "Never piss off people who can promote you, fire you, or make things difficult for you. Therefore, don't hack anything because somebody might get upset."

Yet when we compared their reactions with reality, we found that this fear was absolutely unjustified. Out of over four thousand benevolent hacking case studies we reviewed—specifically, situations where someone worked around stupid procedures and barriers—only three hackers reported ever getting fired because of their hacks. (Two admitted they did end up doing some harm—thus not truly benevolent hacking—and one said his boss was looking for any excuse to fire him anyway.)

**That's a 0.075% chance of getting fired for hacking your work.** Your house is six times more likely to be hit by lightning than you are to be fired for hacking benevolently! Though we expect the publication of this book to increase the number of slightly more risky hacks, so far hacking work has had a very safe record. And as long as you stay within what we're calling benevolent hacks, fears about other negative impacts, like a slower career track or bosses making life more difficult for you, appear to be baseless. Even leaders who argued in favor of those fears couldn't back them up with concrete examples.

One leadership coach told us that no one in his right mind would hack his work, especially not in a tough economy. "Too risky," she said. Yet later in the same email exchange, she admitted, "I routinely work around standard processes, as do all of my colleagues. That is the reality of the workplace, as it has been for as long as anyone I have talked with can remember, and that's going back at least eighty years. It is definitely easier to do with Internet access, but [hacking] isn't anything new."

So if this underground army has at least an eighty-plus-year history, including some, if not most, of today's leaders—where are the mass firings? Why should anyone avoid hacking?

Answer: There is no good reason. Hack away!

Of course, to cover our butts, our lawyer insisted that we insert this disclaimer: Our interview results do not guarantee your results. As always, caveat emptor—or as hackers might say, your mileage may vary.


## THE NEW RULE

Playing by the rules has changed. Keeping your nose clean and following your boss's rules used to keep you secure and employed. No longer. Here are two old rules that force us into a new one:

1. **All work should serve higher purposes.** Happy customers, bosses, and shareholders; rewarding and enjoyable team-mate relationships; personal growth and development; the joy and rewards that come from accomplishment and challenging oneself; a secure future for you and your family. Every day is a juggling act of managing multiple, and often conflicting, higher purposes.

2. **All systems currently default to company priorities.** Most everything that's built for you to get your work done defaults to only one set of higher purposes: company results and how the company wants things done, leaving you to work way too hard accomplishing everything else that is important to you. Until business gets the need to be user centered, that forces you to follow new rule three. . . .

3. **If your priorities are pushed too far into the background, or are too hard to achieve, you must change the default setting.** That means you must hack your work, changing the tools and procedures you use so they default to include your needs—making it as easy for you to succeed as it is for the company. Again, this does *not* mean sticking to the Man, but rather improving your situation so you can do your best for everyone.

This is where the last elephant in the room appears. It's not fear or protecting the status quo. It's being responsible. While virtuous and noble in intent, this one also deserves closer examination.

We all want to do the right thing. And since we discovered in school that hacking was bad—tsk, tsk—and that the right way is to always follow the rules and pay attention to the authority figure, then being responsible must mean doing what we're told to do and not questioning the boss.

From childhood, we've been trained that being responsible and following the rules are the same thing. That means that if you're stuck with IT procedures that weigh you down, and you're being responsible, you're not supposed to jump the firewall. And that no matter how it hampers your personal productivity or effectiveness, you're supposed to perform every procedure exactly the way the company says and use every tool the company hands you.

Like hell. Even the company suffers if you play by those rules.

Jensen Group research into this problem found that companies, customers, and employees are being hampered by doing what we're "supposed" to do every day. Survey results from over fifty-five hundred midmanagers across the globe found:

- ► Corporate-supplied tools and processes reduce personal productivity by 30–75% (compared with what's available outside of work).
- ► 92% of those surveyed believed that those daily inefficiencies had a direct impact on their team's ability to solve problems and innovate.

Being responsible means recognizing that it's sometimes more important to do what's right than to do what we're supposed to do.

We all have personal stories to back up these findings. For example, one master trainer we know was conducting a class on advanced project management techniques. The most popular discussion of the day was on the "corporate sins" the students regularly committed in order to get things done. Most common for this group: speeding up the procurement process by bypassing the procurement guys on their end and the sales and marketing guys on the vendor's side. The group concluded this simple hack easily and consistently cut 50% off the total time spent on a project.

These "sinners" swore that they could document that they maintained high ethical and due diligence standards. A 50% reduction in time spent without a single ethical breach or lapse in project standards! And these are not isolated instances by lone wolf anarchists.

# RISK TOLERANCE:
## MAINTAIN A BALANCED HACKING PORTFOLIO

**Like almost** anything in life, there's a spectrum of risk associated with hacking. Risk carries both upsides and downsides. The best approach is to maintain a balanced portfolio of four different risk levels. Playing it too safe could burn you as much as taking too many risks. Since risk is a personal assessment, you need to find the best mix for you:

1. **Life Changing:** High risk, highest reward
   Example: Your hack creates a new product, gives birth to a new company, or changes an entire industry (think Walmart, FedEx, and iTunes).

   Entrepreneurship has always been a game of risk—whether it's your job, your reputation, or your self-regard.
2. **Career Changing:** Moderate risk, high reward
   Your hack changes how your company does things and establishes you as a subject matter expert (for example, the building of BlueShirt Nation for Best Buy; see

These are the acts of scores of certified expert project managers—hard-core lovers of strict procedures—who didn't realize that *all* of them created work-arounds just to get their projects done until they openly shared how they did it.

Playing by the new rules means that you now have an obligation—to the company as well as to yourself—to change the default setting on "supposed to" tools and procedures. Being responsible means exercising a lot more common sense and a lot less blind obedience chapters 5 and 7). The risk? Trying and failing, the same risk that goes with any personal accountability.

3. **Work Changing:** Low to moderate risk

   Your hack bypasses a lousy boss or stupid procedure or corporate-centered tool but unfortunately isn't self-sustaining: You have to repeat your work-around each time (for instance, having to jump over the firewall again and again). While this is where most hacks occur, the ideal situation is to work with your company or teammates to find more sustainable solutions.

4. **Getting By:** Low risk

   You play it safe. You work around procedures only when you know your manager will back you and only when there's almost no possibility of a downside. There's nothing wrong with this approach, except that it does nothing to give you control of your own destiny.

Degree of reward is also a personal assessment. Some hacks will just make that day more manageable, some will forever change your life and the lives of everyone around you. Find the mix that works best for you.

and making sure the company has better ways to do things than what they handed to you.

Which systems, tools, and structures should be spared from hacking because the company's priorities *should* outweigh yours? And which should be changed through work-arounds? That will vary by company, by context. But the debate about whether or not most corporate structures and tools need to be benevolently hacked is over. The stakes are too high for all of us to keep playing by the old rules.

## EVERY "YEAH, BUT . . ."
## COMES DOWN TO ONE THING:
## PERSONAL CHOICE

To hack or not to hack has nothing to do with bosses, job security, rules, or company policies. It all comes down to how you choose to balance your need to control your own destiny with the equally important need to provide a secure future for you and your family. There is no right or wrong choice, there is only your choice.

So, for example, when fifteen-year-old Ari Weinstein and his cohorts released software that helped others "jailbreak" their iPhones—enabling them to download programs not sanctioned by Apple—some would view their choice as too risky. (Even though jailbreaking is becoming more mainstream: The first instructional jailbreak video for Apple's new iPad was posted on the Web within hours of its release.)

But when Athanasaki, a project manager from Greece, bypasses his IT help desk and approaches IT staffers directly, most would categorize this choice as significantly less risky. His company's policy is that every employee should call the help desk anytime there's an IT problem. That typically means a three- to five-day wait for a fix. Athanaski's work-around is to track down a friendly IT staffer in the building for an immediate fix.

If you're tempted to give in to unhealthy fear, remember to start small and work your way up. KISS! While some of the most progressive and useful hacks come from those who blatantly ignore the rules, workmanlike (and relatively safe) hacks like Athanasaki's are the ones that keep business's wheels from coming off day in, day out.

If you believe that hacking will get you in trouble, it probably will. Fear will win out no matter how many successful case studies we put in this book. However, if you believe that it's truly crucial and urgent for you to take more control of your own destiny, you will find ways to hack that are safe enough for you. It's that simple.

Regardless of whether you're fearful, fearless, or somewhere in between, we'd suggest that you explore hacking to discover more about yourself. Learn more about finding the best balance for you between control and security. What you discover may surprise you.

Benevolent hackers believe that fixing things so they work better for everyone serves a higher purpose. And that's what got them past the elephant in the room.

## WORK-AROUNDS FROM THE FIELD

**Put Your Ass on the Line Within Thirty Days** from Matthew Milan: "A few years back I joined a large digital agency, as an experience designer. Because it was all digital, my team of twenty-five was inexperienced and quite young. This was a challenge, as they were tasked with telling much older executives what they should do with the Internet. They tried managing us the way they managed everything else—with lots of formality, tightly controlling our relationship with the clients. They saw us as a bunch of bratty kids. One executive said right to my face, 'You guys frustrate me. I don't know what the fuck you do or how you do it.'

"They threw up their hands and put me in charge while they searched for someone to take over our group. **Hacking lesson one:** Act like a leader who has the authority to change things, whether or not it's been granted. I looked outside our team for ideas and discovered the thinking of Jeanne Liedtka from the University of Virginia's Darden Graduate School of Business. She says most innovation happens as a result of end runs around problems . . . hacking!

*(continued)*

Based on the ideas of Liedtka and others, I started with our end runs—working backward from our team's needs and working toward the company's needs—the exact opposite of the way it's usually done. I mapped everyone's individual needs; I did interviews on how we thought we could create value for our clients; discussed what we thought the management team needed to see from us; brainstormed what fast goals we should set for ourselves and the tools and approach we'd use to get it all done. **Hacking lesson two:** Be user centered—design from the bottom up, not the top down.

"**Hacking lesson three:** Tools matter. We ignored the company's knowledge management initiative and used a wiki to build our ideas and solutions. We started using Twitter as our main communication tool. We started tackling client problems fast—things that used to take weeks we turned around in hours, because we weren't burdened by how things were *supposed* to get done. Within thirty days, one of our SVPs came back from a companywide meeting and others had told him that we were among the best business strategists in the company. Nice compliment, but not true. All we did was solve problems within the right time scales. With all their structured ways of doing things, our bosses couldn't do that.

"**Hacking lesson four:** Produce, and nonbelievers become sponsors. Suddenly, that SVP was blocking for us and removing barriers. People inside the company started fighting over who got first access to our expertise and information. We went from [being] the most inefficient group in the company to the most efficient; staff morale went from poor to excellent; and we were given seats at the strategic table. Most important, clients started paying us for our thinking, not the hours we worked."

# MAKING A DIFFERENCE

Power . . . Control . . . Risk.

The unspeakables.

Hacking work breaks these taboos
and focuses the conversation on
one simple question:
"How easy is it for me to do great work?"

Exploring that question forever changes
how we all get on with the work of doing
what really matters.

# 10

# DEAR BOSS ...

> Change is still made by people with some sort
> of authority. It's driven by managers who have a
> platform to advocate for a new direction and the
> ability to hire, promote, and reward those who
> embrace it.
>
> —Jack Welch, former CEO, General Electric

## WHAT HACKERS WANT BOSSES TO KNOW
## ABOUT THE NEW WORLD OF WORK

Many who read this book are likely to share Jack Welch's view.

And this is why hackers hack. The opinion of "Neutron Jack"—written just as the severity of the economic meltdown revealed itself in the fall of 2008—is that we "need to acknowledge" that the only ones with the power to safely drive change are those who can hire, promote, and reward those who follow their lead.[1]

That's the kind of thinking that, yes, turned GE into a global powerhouse, but that *also* got us into the economic mess we're in—creating layers upon layers of problems that now need to be fixed at most companies. Including lots of hack-worthy problems at GE.

Since the early 1990s, about a thousand GE workers, midmanagers, and senior executives have participated in the Jensen Group's ongoing study, *The Search for a Simpler Way* (almost all without corporate approval). If those thousand interviews and survey results represent the institution as a whole, then GE could be the poster child for a company whose work tools and processes are failing its employees and deserve to be hacked.

Thanks to its early adoption of Work-Outs, Six Sigma, and myriad other corporate-centered process and performance tools; its performance-driven culture; and its unequaled development of its most senior executives, GE has been one of the world's best-performing companies for decades, including $11 billion in profits in 2009. Even with falling earnings, it still beat Wall Street's expectations for the end of that year. Impressive.

But how user centered are all those high-performing structures?

How easy does GE make it for 320,000 *individuals* in its workforce to do great work? According to those we interviewed, once you get below the people who attend Crotonville, GE's famed leadership academy, GE would rank as one of the most autocratic and corporate-centered, least user-centered companies.

Now, there are caveats (we don't want this behemoth coming after us for defaming them),[2] but consider the moral of this story: There's a possibility of a major gap at a high-performing company between simplicity for the leaders and processes that drive corporate returns and rigid complexity for the people doing the work—imagine! Who'da thunk it? This is exactly why it's important for leaders to learn from their hackers to change how they build infrastructures.

## FREE-AGENT CHANGE AGENTS

The best hackers would be in complete agreement with former CEO Welch in how he defines a change agent: "First, true change agents see a future no one else does, and that vision won't let them rest. . . .

Second . . . change agents are willing to take bold action—and accept the consequences. . . . Finally, change agents have something about them that galvanizes teams and turns people on. . . . Most have a fervent core of supporters, cultivated through intensity and caring. . . . In the end, you know a true change agent when you see their people buy into a change effort not to avoid punishment but to reap its great reward."[3]

That's exactly how the great hackers that we interviewed see themselves and their hacks! Put any great business leader and any great hacker together and ask them what it takes to be a change agent, and the event would be a love-fest.

So where's the dividing line between them?

It's the power structure. Mandated tools, infrastructure, processes, and procedures—the very things the institution uses to boost efficiencies, productivity, and results for the *institution*—that do not pay equal attention to the burdens, extra work, and inefficiencies those corporate-centered designs force upon each *individual*.

The rift between the two sides of this issue is how tools and structures are used and who gets the most benefit from them. When an individual's or team's or customer's needs are ignored, then hackers feel they must act like free agents for change—creating workarounds to fill those gaps. Why? Because from the hacker's point of view, they were broken when sent to him.

Like Rom Feria, a distinguished faculty member at the University of the Philippines. His hacks are focused on teaching styles that do not match students' learning styles and mandated courseware that cannot be adapted to either the students' or the faculty's needs. Like Jack Welch with his description of a change agent, Feria attracted a fervent core of supporters who are reaping a great reward—but his followers do so by turning their backs on centralized systems and turning to open source courseware. He began by promoting open source solutions, software that can be freely modified by students and faculty alike, throughout Philippine universities and colleges. Today, the same courseware is being used in Brazil, Indonesia, and Vietnam.

"Those in power must realize that this is the participation age— where users are no longer just spectators but also coauthors and redesigners," says Feria. And to his credit, in a magazine column eight months later, Welch somewhat agreed: "To be someone else's employee, people are telling us, is to be at someone else's whim. . . . Something fundamental in our society has changed, and it will show up in how people choose their next jobs. . . . [A] brave new type of employee will rule the day. And only brave new companies will be able to entice them back."[4]

## DEAR BOSS:
## FIVE BIG IDEAS WHERE YOU SHOULD BE
## LISTENING TO THE WISDOM OF HACKERS

To survive everything that the marketplace throws at you and still thrive, you're going to have to become a brave new company. Hackers can help you . . . if you can embrace two things about them. First, they won't make your life easy. They'll challenge most of your preconceived notions and counsel you to do things that will scare the shit out of you. Second, that's exactly why you need them. They will push you to places you need to go—and get you there ahead of your competition. If you're willing to learn from the hackers within your midst, you'll kick the competition's butt and satisfy customers more. Guaranteed.

Nothing that needs to change is your fault. It's the system's fault. It's not meeting your needs or those of your employees. But who is the key decision maker on how those tools and processes get built? Yup, you. So the fault may not lie with you, but accountability does. That's why they pay you the big bucks.

# DEAR BOSS:
## FIVE BIG IDEAS TO SAVE YOU FROM YOURSELF

1. **User-Centered Design Moves from Marketplace to Workplace:** Make it as easy for your people to do great work as you do for your customers to buy your products.

2. **ROI Gets Personal:** Your work contract must finally get real.

3. **Training and Development Finally Become Learner Centered:** Developing each person in ways that work best for him or her creates amazing returns.

4. **The Org Chart Marries Social Network Maps:** Your leadership pipeline has been democratized.

5. **The Art and Science of Clarity Move from Marketplace to Workplace:** You can no longer take for granted that everybody knows how to communicate to everybody.

# BIG IDEA 1:
# USER-CENTERED DESIGN MOVES FROM MARKETPLACE TO WORKPLACE

**What's got to change?** The belief that your company has the right to use employees' time and attention as you see fit. This core assumption is driving much of what's wrong with work design today.

**Critical first step.** Ask hackers to help you evaluate whether your current tools and processes are user centered. (Which you'll never see or accept unless you change your core assumption.)

**Success.** When your employees can answer "Yes" to "It's easy to do great work here."

ANYONE WHO'S EVER HAD A GREAT CUSTOMER EXPERIENCE recognizes this scene, from a customer's video posted on YouTube: "Hey, everyone, I wanted to tell you about my new kitchen floors that I got from Lowe's. We got this new refrigerator that Lowe's put in . . . [but] they didn't hook it up correctly . . . so water ran all over our floor and ruined it. . . . I called Lowe's . . . and they were *so* nice.

"Jeff was the manager and . . . he [installed] a brand-new wood floor! It's gorgeous, it's beautiful, it's everything I ever wanted. . . . I just want to say thank you to Lowe's for the nice job . . . and the great customer service. . . . Thank you!"

We all want Jeffs in our corner! Yet what's important to realize is that Jeff couldn't have delighted his customer without an infrastructure that made it easy for him to immediately locate replacement flooring, and made it easy for him to reallocate staff to install it, and made it easy to do so at no cost to the customer. All those "easy to" steps were made possible by having customer-focused infrastructure, tools, and processes in place.

That's marketplace user-centered design. That's why Amazon, eBay, Lands' End, and Drugstore.com spend tons of time and money studying how customers use their sites and then make infinitesimal changes that result in gazillions in revenues. That's why Google tested its most recent redesign with hundreds of thousands of users—including all twenty thousand of its employees—before rolling out changes, many of which can only be measured in one-pixel increments. It's all based on working backward from what people need, how they behave, and what works for them.

While the people part of our customer experience will often be the most critical, more and more of the foundation of that experience will be how our needs were built into the supplier's infrastructure. Whether it's at a drive-up window, an emergency room admittance, or how your luggage arrives at the same airport at the same time as you, the design of the supplier's infrastructure is the invisible hand that determines much of our great or lousy experience. The more user centered the design, the better the experience. The more supplier centered the design, the more you feel as though you're doing their work for them—which is *never* motivating or enjoyable.

Companies "get" this when it comes to their customers, and yet . . .

**Somehow, most companies never got the memo on being user centered *inside* their firms.** The overwhelming majority of work systems today are corporate centered, not user centered. This does *not* make these companies *bad*, just ill prepared to fully embrace the New World of Work. And ripe for the benevolent hacking of all their systems. All that hackers want is to have their day-to-day needs built into your infrastructure. Doing otherwise is misusing your most critical resource by wasting people's time, attention, and capability.

An example from our experience—a major missed opportunity for internal user-centered design: A few years ago, Bill was asked to help simplify the training for all branch managers and staff for one of the world's largest banks. This bank had grown primarily through acquisitions and needed to build a new approach to staffing its branches—creating the best possible customer experience that was also cost-efficient.

Part of Bill's research was to talk to more than two dozen branch managers from the newly acquired bank about their biggest day-to-day challenges. The number one challenge at that moment: their email system. They were told that integration of the two banks' IT systems would take the better part of a year before the new system would be fully functional. Meanwhile, they were stuck in communication limbo.

So what did they do? Most branch managers suffered in silence, which meant accepting up to an hour of extra work each day—in additional phone calls and meetings—to make up for the desperately needed IT tools. Time that should have been spent on customers. Four managers started jumping the corporate firewall to use open source services like Gmail (a well-intended hack but, still, probably sharing some information that should have remained within the firewall). All because nobody was focused on their day-to-day needs while the two banks became one.

The hundreds of people working on the staffing model never addressed this problem or half a dozen similar problems at the branch level. Because even though they truly cared about every person in every branch, ultimately they were accountable only for corporate-centered designs: the most cost-effective ways to staff the branches and train them in the new approach.

None of this makes the company's approach wrong. But the problem, as discussed in chapter 6, is that there are always *two* sides to the challenge.

Somebody also needed to be focused on user-centered problems, such as months-long IT switch-overs, that would impact every branch manager's *personal* productivity. Somebody needed to be focused on how the staffers wanted and needed to work rather than forcing them to accommodate the designer's approach. That didn't happen.

**If most companies are not bad, and want to do right by their employees, why does this keep happening? Why is so little of their design user centered?** It all comes down to one core assumption, an industrial age holdover: the right to mandate how time and attention will be used.

Because companies believe they have the right to use employees' time and attention as they see fit, they keep being company centered in everything they build, assuming that they have eminent domain over how employees need to work. They see this as part of the employment contract. Thus, no compelling reason to be user centered.

Well, over the past decades, especially in the past couple of years, employers have broken almost every bond on their side of the contract, yet this assumption still remains. What needs to finally change is your eminent domain assumption about your right to mandate how an employee's time and attention will be used.

Like it or not, the implicit contract you have with every worker is now governed by the immutable laws of the "attention economy." We are living through the largest increase in expressive capability in human history—most employees now have the tools and opportunities to seize complete control over what they pay attention to. And where their attention goes, so go their time and energies. And where their time and energies go, so goes their productivity. You can still guide, focus, and reward them for how their time, attention, and energy get spent, but you lost *control* over those things a long time ago.

Once you change that one eminent domain assumption, suddenly building user-centered infrastructures becomes a critical business imperative. Changing your assumption means that the right to use people's time and attention must be *continually earned* and is not forever signed away by them just because they work for you.

What happens otherwise? You lose your best employees—either through departure or through disengagement . . . they're there only until they can find their next job.

How to solve this? Ask your hackers. They're your best teachers for how to continuously earn everyone's time and attention. (We'd prefer you listen to them, but if you want specific next steps from us, see chapter 11.)

## BIG IDEA 2:
## ROI GETS PERSONAL

**What's got to change?** The employment contract—the implicit and explicit covenant between you and the workforce. It stopped benefiting all parties a long time ago.
**Critical first step.** Speak the unspeakable: that even though it benefits you greatly, the current contract is not sustainable.
**Success.** When your company starts treating employees as investors.

BEYOND PAY AND BENEFITS, beyond "I work to live, not live to work": Nearly every conversation about the employer-employee relationship ends up spiraling down the same rabbit hole because no one changes the core assumption—that the contract between workforce and company is either a salaried or freelance "work for hire" agreement.

This assumes that one side provides labor and, in return, the other provides compensation and sometimes benefits. And in theory (don't laugh too hard), both sides are able to make plans based on their relationship lasting longer than a nanosecond.

That contract died decades ago, yet few leaders are willing to admit it and change their business plans, structures, and retention efforts according to the current realities.

Admit it or not, you either expect your workforce to work as *investors* or you've been reaping the results of their *behaving* that way for decades but not rewarding them accordingly.

You keep cutting their resources, raising the bar on *morebetterfastercheaper*, and expecting them to make up the difference by investing more of their day and more of their life to help you succeed. You cut your costs and expect them to invest their ideas (intellectual property) and sweat equity to make up the difference. You make mistakes in the marketplace and expect them to cover your investment failures by giving up some or all of their entitlements. They can't get done all they're supposed to in a reasonable workday, so they steal time from their families and invest it in your company.

And what do they get in return? Being able to keep their job for another week? A whopping 0.0001% cost-of-living increase? The joy of living through yet another one of your performance reviews?

It's time to acknowledge the employee-employer relationship for what it really is—an investor-producer relationship. The workforce invests their assets in you, you produce the goods that go to market, and you should be expected to provide a fair and appropriate return back to the workforce on their investments. Here's how that plays out in the **new work contract:**

# Article 1.
## Our working capital gets stuff done.

You (the company) use our assets—time, attention, ideas, knowledge, passion, energy, and social networks—to make your company go. The new contract is all about how to leverage our (the workforce's) working capital and how not to.

# Article 2.
## Our work is an investment.

Our time and attention are finite, becoming more valuable and sought after with each tick of the clock. We choose whether to invest our experience, knowledge, passion, and energy and how much to invest. And the social networks we use to get stuff done are the friends and teammates whose trust we have earned. Every day/week/month/quarter/year (up to both of us to negotiate which is most appropriate), we expect to see returns on these investments. Tell us again: Why should we invest all these assets in you?

# Article 3.
## We want the best possible return on our investment.

If an hour invested in your firm could be invested in a competitor for greater return, your best people will leave to make that investment. If you want us (your best people) to stay with you, here is how we're thinking about ROI:

- ► How easy it is for us to make a big impact
- ► How much of our time is spent doing great and important work and how much of it isn't
- ► How much and how fast we learn
- ► How challenging, rewarding, and exciting our work remains

- How much personal success and balance we achieve—however we choose to define these things
- How well, or poorly, you use the assets we provide

And you don't get to decide those things for us. We get to evaluate you on whether or not you underperformed, met, or exceeded our expectations in these areas. Compensation and benefits are merely baseline starting points for our ROI, based upon what the market will bear, and definitely not the whole return. For most of us, the highest possible returns on our investment will come from areas beyond comp/benefits/options—areas whose values we define, not you.

## Article 4.
## Hello, value—or good-bye.

Our need to get the best possible returns on our working capital forces new criteria into the employment contract. Leadership and the company are middlemen between us and our teammates, customers, and the marketplace. Our exit criteria are no longer just warm and fuzzy issues like feeling appreciated. Middlemen must add lots of value or we dump them. Fast. How much value are you building into our ROI? Can you deliver a more robust and sustainable ROI than we could get on our own or with one of your competitors? That will drive our decision as to how long we'll stay with you and whether to keep investing in you. That will also drive our decision about whether your company becomes our company.

(These are the first four of twenty articles.[5] For more, go to HackingWork.com and download "The New Work Contract.")

**Thinking of your employees as investors may scare you** and create howls of protests. Get over it. Because once you do, you'll see a future of limitless possibilities with a workforce that will work harder, smarter, and faster than anything your competitors can harness.

And you'll see that in order to deliver on your portion of that work contract, almost everything inside your company *has* to be a lot more user centered. That's how employees will get the returns they need on their time, attention, knowledge, and more.

Business is still dragging its collective feet on updating the work contract. There is no exemplar for its complete adoption. But there are lots of success stories for partial adoption. . . .

Employees of San Francisco–based Skyline Construction participate in a pick-your-salary plan, which allows them to dial down base compensation and ramp up other benefits and personal returns. Genentech, 3M, and Google allow employees to spend up to 20% of their time on projects of their own choosing—increasing personal ROIs for those employees as well as potential innovations for the company. Tech giant Cisco's CEO John Chambers initiated a radical reorganization—senior leadership is now a network of councils and boards with far-reaching authority—making it a lot easier for everyone in the organization to make a big impact and contribute big ideas. Grocery store chain Wegmans has been among the top five of *Fortune* magazine's "100 Best Companies to Work For" for six consecutive years—in part because of its flexibility in scheduling. Retailer Best Buy threw out the time clock for many of its employees, focusing instead on results, not when people showed up.

The common theme behind all these success stories, behind the shift to seeing employees as investors and increasing their ROIs, is giving them greater control of their own destiny. Employees must have greater control over how they contribute and what they get in return—far more personalized for each individual than it is today. Technology enables much of this shift. Mostly what's missing is leadership's will to act—to create and live by the new contract.

Make this shift and you're entering the New World of Work. Hackers will be your buddies. They can show you how best to meet your financial targets *and* deliver greater ROIs to all your employees—and your shareholders.

But if you don't make this shift, you'll leave hackers no other choice. Their work-arounds will focus primarily on building their own ROIs, and they'll stay underground, eliminating your chance to team with them and focus on the company's needs.

Worse, many hackers are investing their efforts outside your company instead of in you. They're figuring out that their hacks are actually products and services that can be sold to others. Your constraining HR policies are right now launching a one-person management consultancy. Your IT procedures are right now launching scores of new tech products and small businesses. All developed by your soon-to-be ex-employees.

And your lathe operator, who you figured had no place else to go, just bumped into one of those techies in the cafeteria. Together, they're investigating how to do rapid prototyping for small manufacturers in the region. They discovered that on-demand manufacturer Zazzle.com can help them produce anything from sneakers to milled machine parts, all without their having to maintain manufacturing facilities or overhead. No threat to your business, maybe, except that you're about to lose an extremely loyal employee who's been with the company forever. Even if that venture never takes off and he stays with you, you've forever lost his head, heart, and any extra "do it for the team" effort.

Many of your best employees—disgruntled because you're not treating them like investors—are actively investing in themselves instead of you.

## BIG IDEA 3:
## TRAINING AND DEVELOPMENT
## FINALLY BECOME LEARNER CENTERED

**What's got to change?** How you train and develop people. You're not getting the results that you need throughout the entire organization.
**Critical first step.** Speak the unspeakable: that even though it keeps costs down, your current approach just isn't effective.

## UPENDING CONVENTIONAL WISDOM

**W**alk into a senior team meeting. Say nothing. Play the video "Lost Generation," found on YouTube—it will take less than two minutes.

Get the team past the fact that it focuses on Gen Y. The key facilitation point is how the video reverses itself. The scrolling text is today's conventional wisdom. Then the scrolled text runs in reverse and every conventional view is upended. Discuss: "Are we ready to reverse conventional wisdom just like the video?" If your senior team is not ready, point out that the workforce will not wait for them. As the voice-over says: "I realize this may be a shock, but I can change the world."

**Success.** When your people are truly your most sustainable competitive advantage.

FANNY SALO, AGE SIXTEEN, MAY HOLD THE KEY to your future as a viable business. She's a Finnish high schooler who gets straight A's and helps lagging classmates while waiting for them to catch up to her.

But "lagging" is a relative term in Finland. According to the Organization for Economic Cooperation and Development (OECD), a group funded by thirty countries to monitor social and economic trends, Finland's students score first in science and second in math and reading—besting the rest of the world.

Their secret? Fanny and her peers get lots of personalized, tailored attention and instruction. The Finnish educational system has the benefit of being greatly subsidized, but funding doesn't solve everything. "In most countries, education feels like a car factory. In Finland, the teachers are the entrepreneurs," creating lesson plans to fit each student, says Andreas Schleicher, who supervises OECD's testing.[6]

Whether you use super-cost-effective technologies or lots of one-on-one mentoring is not the issue. What is: building learner-centered training and development efforts for everyone, not just those in the privileged succession-planning pipeline.

Face it: The development of your people is your only sustainable competitive advantage. Countries and companies alike are realizing that their future truly depends on highly developed human capital. And you know that your efforts, especially in a down economy, aren't anywhere near where they have to be.

Layer that demand on top of statistics that tell the story of the workforce's preparedness, and you've got a ticking time bomb:

- ▶ The ability to use and interpret complex documents is essential in today's global economy. Yet few countries are producing the numbers of students needed who have high-level document literacy—where readers can make complex inferences from extremely detailed material. Norway tops the list; the United States is in the middle.[7]
- ▶ Even though the United States is key to the overall economy, it sits only in the middle as measured by most global scores in reading, math, and science. It does not bode well in a knowledge-based economy when one of the biggest drivers of the economy is only a C+ to B- country.[8]
- ▶ Less than one-quarter of new managers, 23%, get the effective coaching or training they need when they step into a leadership role. Just under 30% of developing leaders (vice presidents and directors) receive the coaching and development they need.[9]

**The time for a major shift is now! Personalized education:** "Societies are looking for ways to make quantum leaps in the speed and efficiency of learning. So long as we insist on teaching all students the same subjects in the same way, process will be incremental," says Howard Gardner, acclaimed author of many books on education and professor at Harvard Graduate School of Education. "But now for the first time it is possible to individualize education—to teach each person what he or she needs and wants to know in ways that are most comfortable and most efficient [for the learner], producing a qualitative spurt in educational effectiveness."

Gardner concludes, "Wherever and whenever personalized education takes hold, the resulting world will be very different. Many more individuals will be well-educated because they have learned in ways that suit them best."[10]

**The power of personalized learning and development is possible now.** All that's missing is a major user-centered "Aha!" and the leadership will to act on it. The business results will be there. The costs can be justified. The solutions will include a mix of cost-effective technologies and one-on-one coaching. All this and more was discovered and proven by shipping giant UPS.

In 2004, when the oldest of Gen Y'ers started applying for jobs, UPS noticed a serious decline in key performance indicators. Teaching their "340 methods"—a detailed manual of rules and routines—through lectures just didn't work anymore. Previous new hires took about 30 days to become proficient drivers. Gen Y'ers were taking 90 to 180 days. Since this generation would soon make up over 60% of the company's part-time loader workforce, if they didn't act quickly, this shift could dramatically impact their bottom line.

Their big "Aha!" was when they recognized the need to reinvent how it taught these new performers—personalizing every step of every tutorial to meet the needs of each individual driver. The company invested more than three years overhauling its training. It didn't lower its standards; instead it built learning-centered training. Teams of UPS executives, professors, design students at

Virginia Tech and MIT, forecasters from the Institute for the Future, and animators all collaborated to work backward from the trainees' needs.

UPS designed video and data-driven proofs of rights and wrongs for each of the 340 methods—providing real-time personalized feedback. In the past, trainees had been expected to accept the wisdom of the trainer at face value. The main training facility in Landover, Maryland, now incorporates a mix of computer-based training, simulations, virtual learning, and self-study. Nearly 85% of the program consists of hands-on learning. As of mid-2010, over seventeen hundred drivers had been trained in this new approach, and results have exceeded expectations in all three of the program's primary goals: enhanced driver safety; decreased new driver turnover; and accelerated time to proficiency for each driver.[11]

Your training and development solutions needn't be that elaborate. They can be as simple as everybody getting a mentoring buddy or free online tutorials from anywhere on the Web with personalized follow-up meetings with internal coaches.

A recent study by consulting firm PricewaterhouseCoopers found that almost every young new hire they surveyed said that working with strong coaches and mentors was critical to their personal development, yet "most businesses only provide coaches and mentors to their senior employees," said Michael Rendell, global head of human resource services at PwC.[12]

There is simply one undeniable law when it comes to the training and development of your people: Personalized, learner-centered education for everyone is the only approach that will yield the outcomes you need. And that's all that hackers are trying to do: personalize what you keep trying to standardize.

## BIG IDEA 4:
## THE ORG CHART MARRIES SOCIAL NETWORK MAPS

**What's got to change?** Your sole ownership of building and nurturing your leadership pipeline.

**Critical first step.** Speak the unspeakable: that your current approach to building your organizational chart just isn't working.

**Success.** When you start listening to Ralph, your part-time new hire, and everyone connected to him.

THE FIRST WAVE OF CHANGE IS ALREADY COMPLETE: One of the earliest success stories in modern social mapping was during the 1980s, when the Centers for Disease Control in Atlanta, Georgia, tracked the social network of Gaëtan Dugas, a French-Canadian flight attendant. Dugas became known as "Patient Zero" for his infamous and pivotal role in spreading the AIDS virus across North America.

Now, whether it's eHarmony, MySpace, Facebook, LinkedIn, Twitter, or scores of other Web 2.0 applications, the verdict is in: Technology's ability to connect people and then map and enhance those connections has been commercialized and is growing more powerful and useful every day. "When I started network research twelve years ago," says Columbia University sociologist Duncan Watts, who's currently on leave from academia to work with Yahoo! Research, "we had virtually no data." Now, hundreds of millions of networked friends provide a constant stream. Watts says this flood of data could be as transformative as Galileo's telescope was for physical sciences: "It gives us a new understanding of our world and ourselves."[13]

And that new understanding has begun to move inside companies. . . .

MWH is a $1 billion engineering firm based in Broomfield, Colorado, that began using social network analysis in 2003. Victor Gulas, who runs both IT and HR for the firm, started using it "to make the invisible visible," he says. His first findings revealed a common problem: that information flowed well within each of the firm's locations, but not between them. He created targeted fixes, such as hiring executive coaches for key senior executives and sending less well known workers on trips to other offices, and then remapped how everyone was connected. After five years, he reports multiple successes: It now takes workers 2.4 steps to get needed information, down from 3.2 in 2003; and technology costs dropped to 3.6% of revenue, from 5.6% six years earlier.[14]

Similar results are reported by every firm currently using social network analysis, says Rob Cross, a University of Virginia management professor. He leads a group of around a hundred companies testing the technology, including Microsoft and Pfizer. He recently asked employees of about twenty companies to identify teammates who helped them perform better; about two-thirds of the names weren't on the firms' previous lists of top performers. Two-thirds!

Given results like that, combined with the ever-dropping costs of technology, if you're not already following Pfizer and MWH's lead, you soon will be. But mapping the connections to improve communications and identify key contributors is just a baby step compared with what needs to happen next. . . .

**It's time for the next wave: marrying the power of social network mapping to your org chart.** Everyone wants leaders they can look to for guidance and inspiration as well as someone to hold accountable for bottom-line results. So social networks won't change your need for some form of hierarchical reporting structure. All that's changing is the selection process, which simply got democratized.

Let's get real here: Everybody in the trenches knows more than you about who their day-to-day leaders are—and they've *always* known the two-thirds of real leaders you've been missing. What social network analysis changes is your ability to find them. This tool now allows you to see all the amazing leaders and high performers who have previously been invisible to you.

The biggest challenge you'll face is not in using the technology—it's in changing your view of how leadership selection works. You thought you had designed the perfect pipeline that would tell you who your next vice president would be. Now, you need to come to terms with the truth that Ralph, the part-time tech support guy, and everyone connected to him may know better.

So along with your formal evaluations, leadership candidate identification, and succession-planning processes that were designed by HR wonks decades ago and are now sucking wind, you need to find and study the hidden networks within your organization. Like Ralph's. Social networking doesn't destroy your need for a formal hierarchy; it just completely reinvents the pipeline that feeds into it.

This is one of the ultimate forms of forbidden innovation that hackers have been practicing. They can easily tell you how to reinvent your pipeline; you've just never invited them to the party. Do so, and learn how many leaders you *really* have, who they are, where they are, what skills they already have, and how best to leverage those skills. Without the baggage that comes with the dusty HR tools and advice you're currently using.

It's also a perfect example of radical transparency, as defined in chapter 8: Nearly every workplace decision that was once made behind closed doors may now involve everyone, everywhere. Because of this, individuals, teams, and aligned groups of people have a lot more power to influence and change management's decisions than we've seen since the dawn of the Industrial Revolution.

How you select leaders is about to become a lot more organic and dynamic, and a lot more of a meritocracy. And the typical career ladder will also change. Instead of having to follow your prescribed path, your employees will find that more paths are open to them thanks to the workforce's networks. If you're linked into those networks, you'll have a shot at keeping prize employees. Otherwise those social networks go straight out the door—along with all the relationships and networks that they compiled while they were working for you.

It's time to start crowdsourcing your leadership pipeline—changing your selection process to include all the insights you're currently not getting from everyone in the trenches.

## BIG IDEA 5:
## THE ART AND SCIENCE OF CLARITY
## MOVE FROM MARKETPLACE
## TO WORKPLACE

**What's got to change?** Day-to-day communications within your firm must address a paradox: At the same time frontline employees have the skills and tools to teach you a lot that you don't get about how to communicate, they also have major gaps in their critical thinking skills. You both need to learn a lot from each other.

**Critical first step.** Speak the unspeakable: that you can no longer take for granted a most fundamental skill—how to communicate with others and how to build clarity and critical thinking into everything you share.

**Success.** When you start providing the training, tools, and support to achieve a critical business goal: that everyone who works for you knows how to pack the most value into, and get the most value out of, each and every communication.

MAYBE WE SHOULD ALL BE ON RITALIN, a pharmaceutical solution to the problem that everyone in every workplace has ADD (attention deficit disorder)! The attention span of the average worker is that of a gnat, and it's even shorter for executives. Keep that in mind as you consider these snapshots of how we use people's attention at work:

▶ The average worker is losing two to four hours per day trying to figure out the meaning of everything that's coming at him, what to pay attention to, and what to do with that information.[15]

- Three of the top five time wasters in everyone's day all relate to communication.[16]
- The amount of information inside most companies is currently doubling every 550 days.[17]
- The average worker receives about 325 pages of information every day yet needs and uses only about 5 pages of information per day.[18]
- Once every three minutes, the average cube dweller accepts an interruption and shifts her focus, consuming 28% of her day.[19]

And all that's only going to get worse. . . .

Business is now operating within the attention economy, where the value of most information has dropped to nearly zero and the scarcest resources are time and attention. Yet how do most companies still try to communicate? By wasting massive amounts of time and attention, cascading information down the hierarchy and through death by PowerPoint. It's time to stop this madness!

It's long past time to stop following internal rules for clarity and communication and start following the laws of the external marketplace. There's a lot you can learn from YouTube, MySpace, advertising agencies, blogs, open forums, Google, and more. (One of the main reasons Twitter exploded was its 140-character limit.)

Human communication is one of the most complex systems ever created, so there's a lot we could cover. To keep us focused, here are the top two things you could do to save your company from itself:

1. **Train for and develop basic communication skills in every single employee, from the most senior executive to the newest hire.** A 2006 study by the Pew Charitable Trusts found that more than half of U.S. students at four-year colleges and universities "lack the literacy to handle complex,

real-life tasks."[20] While many countries do better than the United States, this is a global problem.

Whether you want to accept this or not, a huge chunk of today's workforce is coming to you without the analytical skills to sort through those 325 pages of communication per day, get it down to just the key 5 pages they need, and then transfer what they know to others. You must deal with this! While everyone knows how to use the tools of this decade, few have full digital age literacy.

And don't go thinking, Ah, but that's crucial only for bench scientists, engineers, and senior executives. Your biggest implementation nightmares throughout your company all stem from daily communication misfires. Personal conflict, lack of role clarity, unclear goals and implementation details, and an infinite number of daily misunderstandings and clarifications occur within those gazillions of emails, meetings, and hallway conversations your employees use to get things done. This problem is huge!

Deep digital literacy as well as universal and timeless communication skills are critical to getting everything done, yet precious few of us come to work with those skills fully developed. You've got a major business gap . . . near 0% of business's training and development deals with these daily communication basics:

▶ Inductive/Deductive Reasoning: Knowing how to quickly scan, pull, and interpret all the information sent in emails, IMs, and PowerPoint presentations and meetings
▶ Numerical Reasoning: Understanding what's behind the numbers we're sent every day
▶ Organizing and Synthesizing: Knowing how to structure and condense information in order to increase meaning and comprehension for the receiver

▶ Most Value in the Least Amount of Space: From the receiver's perspective (not the sender's), knowing how to provide the most useful information in the least amount of space and time

Yes, this should have been taught in college. It wasn't. Either deal with it through training and development or deal with it through poor work implementation. Because today's information explosion—doubling every 550 days—will soon be doubling every 450, then 350, then 250 days. So *everyone's* ability to apply critical thinking skills in day-to-day communication will become even more crucial.

This will be especially true as Gen Y hits critical mass. You'll then have to deal with the Gen Y paradox: an entire generation of employees with the attitude that they know how to communicate with anybody, anytime, anywhere, and have the tools to back them up, but who need more help with critical thinking than prior generations in pulling meaning and value from all those communications.

Basic communication skills within your firm will be more and more crucial and will either kill you or be the foundation for your competitive advantages. With information so available anywhere and at any time, your best performers will know how to leverage less as more—how to delete or ignore much of what they get and to clarify the few remaining nuggets for everyone around them.

2. **The most important communication patterns will be the ones you don't control. Study them. Learn how to run your business from your workforce.** "We've spent years talking about the value of water-cooler conversations," says J. P. Rangaswami, head of technology for BT, the British telecom giant. "Now we have the ability to actually understand . . . how information and decision-making migrate. We see how

people really work . . . a new class of supercommunicators has emerged."[21]

In the early 1990s, a concept known as "the learning organization," popularized by Peter Senge, revolutionized the field of organizational development. The idea was that as organizations grew, they lost their natural capacity to learn as company structures and individual thinking became more rigid—and that companies needed to adjust to keep themselves learning. Well, all that was before the explosive use of wikis, blogs, tweets, and everything Web 2.0 has to offer. Every day your workforce is reinventing your firm, your staid structures, your rigid ideas. Every day, through hacks and just plain sharing, they exemplify a learning organization. Do you have the courage to learn from their conversations and give them more autonomy based on what you see?

For example, in chapter 8 we warned potential hackers to beware the digital footprint that they are building because it could be used against them, to control them. What if you flipped that? What if you used everyone's digital footprint to provide them greater empowerment and better ways to self-manage?

What if every manager or team got their own toolkit that included social network maps showing:

▶ How their ideas spread throughout the company—or languished and went nowhere
▶ Who is using information that they supplied to solve key business problems
▶ Who is in each network and how networks used information differently
▶ How their own network was interconnected with others

Or what if everyone received their own customer review index, as well as those of all their teammates, and all the indices included everyone's best and worst reviews?

These ideas will certainly scare the bejeebers out of most Boomer managers, but to a late X'er or Gen Y'er, this is just part of radical transparency. These generations are far more comfortable sharing their networks and feedback and figuring out how to leverage them to do their best than previous generations.

Yes, everything we just covered is a paradox. At the exact same time your workforce is growing more skilled at sharing and using information, they also need more help with critical thinking skills and meaning making. Welcome to the digital age! It's your job to see where you can learn from them and from what they're up to and where you need to provide much stronger training and development for them.

**One of the biggest, most strategic ideas** in your competitive arsenal could very well be the simplest and most basic: rethinking your approach to, and upping your investment in, day-to-day communication. And hackers can show you the way. Most of their workarounds are attempts to change your most staid and useless current approaches to methods that work best for them.

## WHAT THESE FIVE BIG IDEAS ADD UP TO

Start learning from, and start thinking like, the hackers in your midst.

Benevolent hackers have one core goal: Make the system work for the people doing the work, not just for the company. This has been your biggest blind spot and leadership weakness for decades. Put these five ideas into practice and you will greatly accelerate all your implementation plans, as well as build the kind of culture where your people are truly your biggest competitive advantage.

# WORK-AROUNDS FROM THE FIELD

**CEOs Are Hackers, Too** from John Girard, CEO of Clickability: "I'm a firm believer in the adage that entrepreneurs are the people who steal office supplies from home to bring to work. All great entrepreneurs are passionate hackers at heart. As an entrepreneur who competes in a fast-changing marketplace, here are some of my favorite work-arounds:

"Creating email folders that contain automatic rules for building meeting agendas. I email myself notes with the right code in it, and the next meeting I have already has a bucket of agenda items ready to discuss.

"Always choosing open, fast, cheap, and simple over the complex. I'd much rather run and track my business in Google Docs than with some big ERP [enterprise resource planning] system.

"Cool tools that let you do cool things. CubeTree brings together all sorts of information I need to run my business and integrates it in ways that expensive proprietary tools still can't do.

"Stand-up meetings. Don't let anyone get comfortable. Have a note taker. Delegate 95%, and don't let anyone leave the table until the other 5% gets sorted out."

## WORK-AROUNDS FROM THE FIELD

**When Restructuring Affects Quality of Life** from Ross:
"When Microsoft moves a team from one office building to another, they distribute worksheets to the occupants of every office to be moved. With the worksheet comes a sheet of stickers with the new office number printed on them, so that every item of equipment can be marked with a sticker indicating its destination.

"My team was moved some years ago from a new, well-appointed building to a shabby backwater. By way of consolation, one of my teammates used his spare stickers to mark up the fancy furniture in the lounge down the hall. When we arrived at the dull new office on Monday, we found that, yes, the lounge had come with us."

# 11

# STOP THE
# MADNESS NOW

I have been impressed with the urgency
of doing. Knowing is not enough; we must apply.
Being willing is not enough; we must do.

—Leonardo da Vinci, Renaissance man

## HOW TO WORK AND LEAD DIFFERENTLY
## IN A HACKED WORLD

There was a chill in the air. Harold pulled tight his cloak and stood
with an entire country at his feet, shimmering with the light of
Halley's comet passing overhead. It was just two months after his
coronation as king of England in 1066, and he was about to be hacked.

Unknown to Harold, the Normans were in Rome petitioning the
pope to authorize a work-around to Harold's claim to the throne.
This was because two years earlier, William, Duke of Normandy, had
saved Harold from a shipwreck and as a reward was promised rights
to the throne. But when it came time to make good on his promise,
Harold decided, "It's good to be the king."

Armed with a work-around proclamation from the pope, William
gave Harold a choice: Accept arbitration by the Vatican or meet him

on the battlefield in Hastings. Harold did not choose wisely. William the Conqueror kicked his butt in battle and crowned himself king on Christmas Day. And the history of business was forever changed.

All that was set in motion because the person in charge, poor Harold, tried to ignore the power of hacking.

History is full of hacks big and small, failed and successful, bloody and uncontested. The one thing many have in common is intense conflict—opponents unable to resolve their differences without one side winning and the other losing.

Can't we all get along?

## THE REAL PROBLEM: POINTING FINGERS AT EACH OTHER

If benevolent hacking is to save business from itself, we're going to have to do it differently from Harold and William. Both sides on the hacking debate have valid views, and both could benefit from the other's insights.

During our interviews, non-hackers and leaders backed their views on hacking work mostly with broad, negative value judgments: "What you're promoting is stealing." . . . "This will excite the mobs to overturn the establishment." . . . "Don't go blaming these failures on lack of leadership. I'm doing what's right; they're wrong." . . . "These hackers are full of themselves. They don't listen to feedback, and they set their standards too low."

The hackers we interviewed understood those concerns but felt that their insights and equally valid concerns weren't being heard. Too many one-way terms of the relationship are being dictated and hidden within those structures and tools. Especially in the midst of an economic meltdown, if their employers won't supply what they need to do their best, they can't sit idly by with their hands tied. They felt compelled to create what's needed.

Yet they're not blameless in the antagonism and lack of transparency that swirls around benevolent hacking. You've seen how few people we could get to stand behind their hacks with full name and title attribution. As one anonymous hacker admitted, "It takes cojones to publicly confront the system. I don't know if I'm up for that."

And as with everything in life, there's hell to pay if well-intentioned hacks are done poorly. Said one who's cleaning up after a hacker's mess, "One of our directors tried to hack our performance management form, which I admit was a piece of crap, but he ended up with a bigger piece of crap! He mandated that everyone in his division use his new form. Yes, his hacking attempt did bring the issue to the forefront—only because of what he did, we're now getting a much improved performance management system. That's great. But the guy created a lot of problems for all of us in the meantime."

**The divisiveness must stop!** OK . . . you're both right . . . can we move on now? For hacking to be a positive force, it can't be *us* vs. *them* anymore. We've got to come together as one team.

## HACKS CAN BECOME MAJOR LINES OF BUSINESS

In 1998, long before YouTube, Hewlett-Packard researchers and engineers in Corvallis, Oregon, needed a way to share what they were learning in each of their projects. They began videotaping presentations so they could share insights and innovations with other researchers and engineers from around the world.

"No boss authorized any of this," explained ex-team member John Morris. "So we copied over old videotapes that everyone brought in. A few tapes of children's birthday parties were sacrificed for our team, VidNet. We saved millions of dollars in travel expenses by hacking together a primitive transmission system to share these videos. We had no budget for the only guy on our team who knew how to do that, Mike Vanderford, so we paid him with an unending supply of microbrewed beer."

Fast-forward to early 2008: HP partners with DreamWorks

Animation to produce Halo Telepresence, their new high-end video teleconferencing tool. HP calls upon the VidNet team to leverage ten years' worth of hacked know-how on building cost efficiencies into the system. Vanderford becomes lead engineer. His kid loves video gaming, which is where the product name, Halo, comes from. HP currently sells its Halo Collaboration Studio system for over $300,000 apiece. "And its origin is a cobbled-together hack of duped-over videotapes funded by microbrews," said Morris.

Mike Vanderford added, "Most hackers have such passion for what they do that they don't realize the impact they're having. None of what we did back then was mainstream, and I was lucky enough to work in a great place with visionaries who gave me the freedom to experiment and, of course, who kept those microbrews coming."

Bottom line: Not only does *not* allowing hacks cause everyone lots of lost productivity and create lots of frustration, but *encouraging* them can actually grow the company and make things better for everyone!

## NEW LEVELS OF LEADERSHIP ACROSS ALL LEVELS

In a hacked world, each of us is going to have to take leadership to new levels within our level of the organization.

We're all on the same team with a shared goal of helping business perform better, with different responsibilities. If you're an employee under a manager, hacking will dramatically increase your ability and responsibility to lead from the bottom up. If you are a midmanager, it changes what you need to provide for your team and how much more you can do for senior management. And if you are at the top of the food chain, hacking will ask a lot more of you. How you listen for and respond to the needs of your workforce will change greatly.

The three sections that follow—working, managing, and leading—take you through the changes in responsibilities that hacking brings to each level of your organization.

# AGREE TO BE OFFENDED

**Kyra Gaunt** is an anthropology professor at Baruch College
in New York City. She has led workshops around the world
titled "Agree to Be Offended." While her focus is on creating
connections through conversations about race, the same
applies to hacking. Adapting her course description: When we
find ourselves personally offended by another's views, we are
denying the other party's reality—invalidating it and them.
We need to stay in the conversation long enough to get past
being offended and start seeing how their views are valid.

Regardless of your views on hacking, here are suggestions
for four conversations about how hacking will play a role in
our future. Start these conversations with your teammates,
with your manager, and—if you're a senior executive—with
everyone in the company. Stay engaged long enough to get
past being offended and start discovering new possibilities.

1. **Get Comfortable with Co-created Structures.**
   Hackers change processes and tools without
   permission from someone in authority. What's
   wrong with that approach? What's great about it?
2. **Co-creation Means Redefining Innovation.** Could
   making it safe for everyone to question how things are
   done, simple for everyone to expose what does not
   work, and easy to co-author new solutions drive
   completely new levels of innovation and productivity
   within our company?
3. **Co-creation Means a New Shared Code of Ethics.** To
   what ethical practices should all parties in this debate
   hold themselves accountable? (Keep in mind

*(continued)*

that solutions cannot be forced or mandated and must
respect all parties' needs and concerns—consensus
can't be dictated from above.)

4. **Business Trusts Vendors and Customers More Than
Its Own Employees.** Is this true at our firm? If so, list
examples of how vendors and customers can change
and influence processes in ways that employees
cannot. Discuss ways to change this dynamic.

(See chapter 8 for more details behind each of these
conversations.)

## WORKING DIFFERENTLY
## IN A HACKED WORLD

This section is just for the hackers who have no formal authority to
change tools and processes: most of us. You may or may not have
some management responsibilities, but primarily you are a producer,
a teammate. The biggest change in your role will be how you can
lead from the bottom up.

Let's begin with the most common advice we heard from midmanagers and senior execs and the absolute worst mistake you could
make if you follow it: "The first and most important thing hackers
need to do is seek senior management buy-in. Getting them to sign
on is critical."

Bullshit.

Follow that advice and you might as well not bother hacking at all.
"Excuse me, sir. I'm going to work around the things you put in place
so you could keep your job, and I'm going to defy your authority to
make me do things your way. May I explain to you why this is a good

thing?" Never gonna happen. Unless you have stumbled upon a truly enlightened senior executive, getting initial buy-in for your hack is unlikely.

*Eventual* leadership buy-in, however, is important. You do want your hack to benefit the entire company, not just you or your team, and those in charge can help you do that. But that's down the road, after your leader has also done her part in embracing the upsides of hacking. Leadership buy-in is her responsibility, not yours. You need to focus on what you can control and influence.

## 1. Deliver Results, Fast!

You've seen this again and again throughout this book: The key to successful hacks is to deliver the goods. Richard Saunders may have hacked his bank's client database, but his senior team loved how he helped them do their job better. Gary Koelling may have advised you to build your own toolkit and avoid your company's infrastructure like the plague, but he also held you accountable: "The key is to start delivering results faster than those corporate-centered results could have."

Every successful hacker said that this was the most crucial priority: Deliver the results your boss and boss's bosses are seeking—*before* they have a chance to get you to do it their way—and all work-arounds will be forgiven, as you'll be helping everyone around you. If you want to stop the madness as well as save business from itself, your top priority must be to deliver great results before those in power have a chance to question your methods.

George Lampere is currently a member of the strategy and transformation practice at Capgemini Consulting. Before that, he had a couple decades of experience in managing large-scale change projects for such organizations as AT&T, NATO, and the U.S. Air Force. He's seen it all.

One of his favorite hacking stories involves an IT development team that preferred to snowboard during the day and then do their best work between 1 and 5 a.m. This did not sit well with their vice president, who wanted them at their desks all day. The VP even went so far as to mandate that they sit where he or others could watch them (they were at several locations) and use the network in a way that would enable him to monitor their online activities.

The team kept disregarding the VP's demand for his arbitrary process, yet he couldn't do anything about it because they kept beating deadlines and outperforming other teams. It wasn't until months later that he figured out how they did it. They found a portion of the network that was underused, reconfigured it for their own purposes, and then used Skype to teleconference with one another when they weren't in the office because the VP wouldn't authorize long-distance charges through the company's phone system.

Despite all the work-arounds and a very pissed-off VP, why was the hack successful and good for everyone? "Because they delivered what really mattered to the company," says Lampere. "Great quality, on or under budget, and on or ahead of schedule."

Deliver the goods as fast as or faster than and as good as or better than the system you're hacking, and everybody wins.

## 2. Out Yourself If Possible, but Definitely Go Transparent.

If hacking is going to truly be a transformative force for business and not just a bunch of one-off unsustainable changes, it's going to have to come out in the open.

If possible, you need to come out. The best way is direct and to the point. Like sitting down with your manager and saying, "You know all those great results I've been delivering? Well, this is how I've been doing it," and letting the chips fall where they may. If your boss embraces your hacks, you've pushed yourself to the head of the class and set yourself up for a promotion. And if not, you probably don't want to keep working there anyway.

Obviously, that may not be best for everyone. Other options include "I have a *friend* who did such and such," masking your own identity; or pulling your team together and having an entire group take responsibility—there's always safety in numbers.

Still, we realize that for many, given most bosses' inability to respond positively, outing yourself may not be possible at this time. However, you do have a responsibility to your teammates, your company, and the rest of us. If you're going to hack and reap the benefits, pay it forward. Post what you've done on blogs and everywhere you can, so others can benefit from what you've learned.

In chapters 6 and 12, we explain how to do that and how not to (never post confidential information; don't expose your company's or people's names) and how to use HackingWork.com as your starting point. Here, we need to mention the importance of transparency.

If we just complain about business's chronic problems and grumble that *they* should change things, every conversation will end with, "Oh well . . ." But if hundreds and thousands of hackers start posting *solutions* to those problems, those hacks will be copied into office email lists, posted in lunchrooms, and passed around during the next team meeting. Suddenly, everybody in the company knows how to work around stupid-work just like you. That puts upward pressure on those who own that stupid-work and forces them into conversations about being user centered, not just corporate centered.

That's the power *and* responsibility that's in your hands. Expose the how-tos of your work-around. Go transparent.

3. **A Hacked World Raises Personal Accountability to Completely New Levels.**

Let's be honest: All those mandated procedures and stupid-work also create lots of places for people to hide. "It's not my job to worry about that. That's So-and-so's job." . . . "I'd love to help you, but the approved process won't let me."

Hacking eliminates lots of those hiding places. Whether that's a good thing or a bad thing depends on you.

According to a recent study by Leadership IQ, an executive performance consultancy based in Washington, D.C., 87% of employees say that working with a low performer has made them want to change jobs.[1] Nobody likes a slacker.

Are you a slacker? If so, you will probably hit a wall in a hacked world. At first, increased hacking by your teammates will seem like a dream come true: "Oh goody, no more stupid stuff!" And then one day it will hit you: "Oh shit, I can't point fingers anymore. There are fewer things to blame." Too bad for you.

For the rest of us . . . fewer hiding places means it's good to be a hacker! Your role and responsibilities will be clearer. Slackers will be less able to call meetings just to create delays, or make excuses, or cite procedures to avoid taking initiative, or push half-completed work back onto your plate. But most important, you will have a clearer, easier path for leading from the bottom up and for proactively managing your career.

Prior to a hacked world, the leaders above you had their own ways to hide—there was a sea of processes, procedures, and reporting structures between you and them. And since all those things were corporate centered, not you centered, the only way your voice was heard in the halls of decision making was maybe through a once-a-year employee survey. And that's so sanitized that it's basically useless. Non-hacked structures are *terrible* listening structures.

In a hacked world, leading from the bottom up is easy. No need to storm the Bastille. Just hack stupid stuff and your results will push things along for you.

Deliver results faster through your hacks than through approved approaches and your leaders will get the message. Not because they want to, but because results matter and because that's how their bosses—customers, shareholders, and the marketplace—keep track of their performance.

## MANAGING DIFFERENTLY IN A HACKED WORLD

Two relentless streams coming at you from opposite directions, often with competing priorities, with you in the middle trying to keep everyone producing and engaged and motivated—that's the role of a manager. Your job is like standing between two funnels with both narrow ends pointed at you. You're accountable for everything leaders shove down at your team—a constant stream through one funnel. And through the other comes every reaction and need that your team would like you to address.

We salute you. You have the toughest job in business!

How does a hacked world help you, and how does it change your role? First, realize that **everything in the previous section also applies to you**. You may need to proceed more carefully than some, because you are watched more closely by execs, but you too can reap the rewards of hacking. Slackers on your team will have fewer places to hide; you will have new ways to fix some of that stupid-work that keeps being funneled at you; and all those work-arounds will mean that you have more time for what really matters—like mentoring and coaching your team and cutting out early for your kid's school events.

Proceeding carefully does not mean no hacking. You just need to continuously get better at managing up. To help with that, in addition to all that's provided here, we've added two free downloads at HackingWork.com: "How to Deal with Managers Who Pile It On: More, More, More, Now!" and "How to Be a Trusted Advisor to Senior Execs." Both are chapters from Bill's book *The Simplicity Survival Handbook*. The core ideas behind each are Soft Hacks—successful ways to negotiate changes in how assignments are handed to you and how you interact with your boss.

But managing up is nothing new. You had to do that in a non-hacked world. The new and biggest change in your role will be in how you interact with your team—providing a safe zone for their hacks. Depending on the degree of risk you're willing to take on (and the degree of reward you'd like to provide back to your team), there are two possible approaches:

### 1. Provide "Air Cover" for the Hackers on Your Team.

"The biggest thing my manager ever did for me," says hacker Amanda, "as big as seven years of mentoring, was to provide air cover for a couple of my hacks. She made sure I was never caught and advised me on how to do it so our team and others benefited. Mentoring me helped me succeed within the company. But providing air cover for my hacks . . . she did just for me, so I could be happy."

Like Amanda, your team may look to you for help in executing their hacks. Air cover can mean advising them on how not to get caught, or helping them network to find other benevolent hackers within the organization, or providing them with additional information or resources. For example, we heard many stories where managers gave their teams dos and don'ts on how to jump the firewall in ways that didn't put confidential information at risk or how to work around a specific procedure but still maintain quality controls. The key element is trust. Your team wants to know, if it's ever necessary, that you've got their back.

Some managers may feel this puts them too much at risk. We hope we've already addressed that feeling in chapter 9— because your team really needs you. They are depending on you to be their advocate, to help create something that is them centered out of everything that is corporate centered. In a hacked world, your role as employee advocate will grow. Until business changes its approach to infrastructure, you will be key to a successful transition into a hacked world.

Does providing air cover still feel too risky to you? That's OK, it's a personal choice. If so, here's another way you can support your team:

## 2. "I See Nothing, I Hear Nothing, I Know Nothing."

In every major change between what was and what shall be, there have always been secret supporters—those who ensure a new future by doing nothing to stop it.

This could include ignoring what you hear as you walk past a conference room, or not asking any follow-up questions when you know the results on your desk came via a hack, or winking at a team leader when you say that you can't "officially" support her approach. The hackers we interviewed said that they preferred to have a manager who was an active advocate, but passive support was also crucial to their successful hacks.

Either way—passive support or proactive air cover—we cannot overstate the importance of your role in the transition to a New World of Work. Eventually, much of the responsibility will sit on the shoulders of those above you. But during the transition, you will be the one keeping your team safe, sane, and motivated.

## LEADING DIFFERENTLY
## IN A HACKED WORLD

Your role is different from the others we've described so far. You have decision-making authority over infrastructure. You may or may not be responsible for why things are being hacked, but you are definitely accountable for leading us into a future where the infrastructure serves everyone's needs equally.

You can no longer authorize the design of corporate-centered tools and procedures and leave user-centered needs unaddressed or as afterthoughts. The stakes are too high for that. For you, for your company, and for everyone.

Here are our recommendations for how to begin to lead differently in a hacked world:

1. **Senior Team Meeting . . . Lock the Doors . . .**
   Confucius said, "To know that you know, and to know that you don't know—that is real wisdom." First you need to admit that you don't fully understand the upsides of hacking; that they don't have to be guarded against, like attacks. Are you willing to look upon benevolent hacking as innovation that has been forbidden for too long? As creative destruction that delivers amazing benefits? You need to be willing to learn what you don't know, learn what no longer serves you, and use these discoveries to come to new conclusions.

   Call a senior team meeting. Lock the doors. Post the following set of five questions on the walls (relating to chapter 10's five things you need to learn from hackers):

   ▶ **Are we willing to build an infrastructure that is as user centered as it is corporate centered?** What are our beliefs and assumptions about our eminent domain rights to determine how plans get executed and how work gets done? Are we willing to change our assumptions? Are we willing to change our tools, procedures, and structures based on what we discover?

▶ **Are we willing to reexamine the employment contract?** (Post on the walls the first four articles of the new work contract, listed in chapter 10.)

▶ **Are we willing to reexamine our approach to training and development?** (Post some of the data points from this part of chapter 10 on the walls.)

▶ **Are we willing to reexamine how we build our leadership pipeline?** (Post some of the data points from this section.)

▶ **Are we willing to admit that improving everyone's day-to-day communication skills is critical to all implementation plans?** (You know the drill by now: Post the data points to focus the debate and facilitate the discussion.)

The only wrong answer to each of these questions is, "No, we're not willing." After that, what matters is exploration: Why does your team hold their current beliefs? Why should they be changed? How urgent is it that they be changed? What's the best way to make the changes?

If you are serious about leveraging the power of benevolent hacking, you and your senior team need to come to new conclusions about the company's eminent domain controls over time, attention, tools, procedures, and infrastructure. Accept this. Be one with it.

## 2. Get Your Fingernails Dirty. . . . Understand Your Infrastructure from a User's Perspective

Soko Morinaga was a Zen master who died in 1995 and was leader of the monks at the Daishu-in temple in Kyoto, Japan. He once said, "Pissing is something that no one else can do for you. Only you can piss for yourself. . . . You must realize that to say, 'Nobody else can piss for you,' is to make an utterly serious statement."

You have no idea how destructive and wasteful your infrastructure is because you don't need to use it the way the workforce does. It's time to stop making someone else piss for you and to realize how much effort it takes to work for you. Drive the forklift, use the database, fill out the form, submit it to HR, and find out how long it takes to get a response. Use your own infrastructure.

In the IT world, using the tools you've designed is called "eating your own dog food" for a reason. Chances are good that you won't like how your own work products taste, and chowing down is the only way you'll know whether or not they're getting any better.

Several years ago, Bill was working with the senior team of a global retailer. Initial survey results showed that senior management's policies and the company's infrastructure were causing lost sales and major implementation problems. Of course, they disputed the results. Those problems couldn't have been their fault. So Bill asked several of the senior team members, including the chief financial officer, to work in a store for a day. The CFO worked as a cashier for a half day—that's as long as he could take.

When it was his turn to present his findings to the senior team, the CFO confessed, "I never realized how hard it is to make money in our stores!" Imagine that. The guy who's in charge of all the money for this company never realized how hard the company made it to quickly and profitably check customers out of the store. And until he sat in a store's break room, he never heard unfiltered feedback from cashiers, stockers, maintenance crew, and store managers about how their tools and processes were affecting them. It was a major wake-up call.

Get your fingernails dirty. Stop relying on survey results and actually use the systems and tools that you force upon your employees. JetBlue's founder and former CEO, David Neeleman, used to do this regularly by working as a flight attendant on JetBlue's flights, and he continues this practice on his new Brazilian airline, Azul—all to better understand what it takes to serve the customers.

You'll never truly grasp the urgency of being user centered until you become that user.

## 3. Change Your Thinking, Change Your Strategies.

In *Through the Looking-Glass*, the White Queen said, "Why, sometimes I've believed as many as six impossible things before breakfast."

Anything is possible once you change how you think about your work structures. Learn from organizations and best practices that revolve around user experiences and excel at being user centered.

A good place to start might be looking into Google's approach. It measures and studies its efforts to be user centered in thousands of different ways: "The Google User Experience team aims to create designs that are useful, fast, simple, engaging, innovative, universal, profitable, beautiful, trustworthy, and personable. Achieving a harmonious balance . . . is a constant challenge."

See the SmartStart box "Learning from Google" for how to meet that challenge. The box covers ten principles that should be applied to all of your processes, work tools, and work structures if you want to become more user centered. Doing so will give you the same competitive edge as one of the fastest-growing, most popular (and free) application suites of all time.

Author and professor Clay Shirky would call Google's ten principles "designing for generosity . . . linking new capability with old motivations through good design."[2] The goal is to build your infrastructure and work tools so they appeal to basic human nature—the need for joy, community, dignity, pride, meaning, and being valued—at the same time as they deliver powerful utility. Everything must be easy to use.

For more assistance, go to HackingWork.com and download "Simpler Companies: A Starter Kit." There we've listed six core measures that will move your tools and processes from corporate centered to user centered, with additional how-to instructions that space does not permit us to publish here.

Whenever you're ready to really dedicate yourself to user-centered infrastructures and tools, the following are suggestions we heard from hackers and executives alike:

▶ Rebuild your leadership development programs to teach leaders how to build user-centered companies (think GE's leadership academy, only designed by benevolent hackers).
▶ At least one senior leader's butt (and bonus!) must be tied to making sure user-centered design gets as much emphasis inside your company as it does for customers.
▶ Create a position on the senior management team or board for frontline workers and midlevel managers—fully invested with the power to ridicule and veto your corporate designs— and then rotate the people in that position periodically.
▶ Build a true meritocracy—where all ideas compete on an equal footing and the best ideas win, where contributions count more than credentials, and where leaders serve rather than preside.

You will come up with even better solutions than those as long as you start with the end user—your employees—in mind. The key to successfully leveraging the power of hacking begins with you changing your views and realizing how many impossible things are now possible.

## 4. Sponsor the Conversation: Change the Debate.

First Lady Eleanor Roosevelt once said, "Do one thing every day that scares you."

Ultimately, your biggest act of leadership will not be studying someone else's best practices or initiating your own. It will be sponsoring and unleashing a different kind of conversation within your company, with you then sponsoring the changes that come out of those discussions.

The most universal fear we found among all senior execs was the act of bringing hacking out into the open. "We'll lose control!"—as if not admitting that all this hacking is occurring means that it doesn't exist. Executives love maintaining the illusion of control. "The mobs will take over the company!"—as if that isn't an indication that leadership has a much bigger problem: If you can't trust your workforce, who's responsible for that? "This is against our values!"—as if providing the workforce with what they need to do their best is against company values.

Open discussion about the merits of benevolent hacking scares most leaders. That's why, at least initially, **leadership in a hacked world comes down to one act: the courage to change the debate.**

You need to make it safe for people to talk about their benevolent hacks. In all our interviews, we saw that within all hackers is an amazing resourcefulness, a sense of imagination, unbridled creativity, and an intense drive to solve business's most chronic problems. They desperately *want* to help you. They want you to succeed. The only reason they've gone underground is that you have not made it safe for them to come out.

Warren Bennis is chairman of the Leadership Institute at the University of Southern California, and his many books are recognized as seminal works on how to lead. One of his most recent, *Transparency*, lays out four critical leadership responsibilities:

► Provide equal access to information.
► Refrain from punishing those who speak the truth.
► Refrain from rewarding yes-men and -women.
► Reward principled contrarians.

Hackers are the next generation of principled contrarians who aren't waiting to speak the truth to power—they're just doing what needs to be done. If they are to help you save your company from itself, you need to make it safe to discuss the possibilities of creative destruction *within* the organization. Make it safe to say that it's necessary to build an infrastructure that serves the people doing the work as much as it serves the company.

Don't worry: You'll get to include tough love in that conversation, too. The more successfully those tools and processes and structures meet the needs of each individual, the greater each person's accountability grows. If tools are better tailored to your employees' needs, you have the right to expect more of them. If employees want the rewards of being treated like an investor, they need to invest more to get more. Guaranteed pay and entitlements could possibly be reduced or tied even more closely to corporate performance. In a hacked world, everybody—up, down, and across—should expect higher levels of accountability tied to performance.

Hackers will keep doing their forbidden innovations with or without your help. But if you'd like their improvements to be scalable and sustainable, if you'd like to use benevolent hacking as a competitive advantage, then you're going to have to change how you lead.

You're going to have to sponsor the conversation that makes it safe for them to come out. Safe for these heroes and their acts to be celebrated.

## NO MORE *US* VS. *THEM*:
## WE NEED TO STOP THE MADNESS TOGETHER

No more finger-pointing. We all own some of the screwups, and we all can contribute to the solutions. We all have responsibilities to some top-down decisions, and we all have increased responsibilities to bottom-up needs and concerns.

### CONVERSATION STARTER

**W**alk in. Link to YouTube. Say nothing. Play "Information R/evolution" by Michael Wesch, Kansas State University—it will take about five and a half minutes.

Some of its content: "There is no top. We organize the information ourselves. It's an information revolution, and the responsibility to harness, create, critique, organize, and understand is on all of us. Are we ready?"

Facilitate a discussion with something like "We'd all agree that the World Wide Web has completely changed how we structure, use, and share information, right? Well, hacking work is doing the same thing to the way company tools and structures are built. Here are some examples. . . ." After examples of hacks: "What are we ready for? What should be critiqued and rebuilt by all of us?"

We need to find a better way to deal with the tensions and competing priorities between individual needs and company needs. Hacking is occurring because our current approach is completely out of whack. The way we build systems to get work done is almost completely corporate centered.

That tension and the need for resolution came through in every conversation we conducted that led to this book. No matter what aspect of hacking people discussed, almost every conversation seemed to bounce back and forth between life, career, family, and company needs. Everybody blurred them all together, bound by a feeling that something just wasn't working the way it should. Nearly everyone was searching for something—better balance, more clarity, less clutter and chaos, more focus . . . something—some better way to handle it all.

For example, take Debbie Rood. She's currently overseeing more than twenty-six thousand employees for Walmart. Before that, she held executive positions in operations for Staples, the Gap, and Toys "R" Us. She was part of our research, where we paired Boomers (Debbie is fifty-five) with Gen Y'ers to discuss what needs to change about how work works. Here's part of her online conversations with Gen Y'er Derek:

"I'm an unusual boss who watches contributions, not the clock. With that said, there does need to be some protocol and structure to stay organized. If you are managing a large team, letting them work 'whenever they want' requires coordination that may not be affordable or reasonable. Taking a call from home late in the afternoon because of a commitment is fine, because you can still orchestrate and accomplish the goals. But it bothers me when folks show up at 9:15 a.m. for a 9 a.m. meeting because they were in the café getting breakfast. . . . It says to me they don't respect the group. . . . I have seen what I feel is a needy person who wants public praise because they completed the assignment—excuse me, that's what you get paid to do. . . . Re tools, technology, and training: My team at the Gap wanted formal training every three months. Yet in my opinion, they didn't take the time to practice and perfect what had already been taught."

Deb also shared life lessons with Derek: "I've raised a Gen Y'er who said, 'You guys work too much . . . I'll never do that.' Well, he didn't have to because we did! I was raised very poor and wanted more for myself. I saw my mother struggle, so I did what it took not to be her. My son watched us work hard, and he is doing what he can to not be us. What are the upsides of working his way? Naturally, his goal is to be a happier person. From a business perspective, does his happiness mean a more productive person? Will he be more loyal? It's nice to believe that all businesses want happy people, but what I've seen is what they want most is to create shareholder value. Happy people need to be more creative, innovative, and productive. I've got more to say on all of this, but right now I have to run to the doctor. Later, Deb."

Right there was real life as it occurs for most of us. Jumbled, streaming, not tightly edited. Tension between personal needs and corporate responsibilities, between corporate-centered structures and user-centered priorities.

Hackers didn't create these tensions. They have existed since the first group of people came together. And hacking won't solve them entirely, either.

Here's what hacking can do: reduce the amount of stupid-work and increase the amount of work that really matters. It can give us all the tools and the power we need to find better solutions. But only if we come together and agree that that's a priority. One team, one shared goal, with different responsibilities to help get us there.

The father of management consulting, Peter Drucker, once said, "Plans are only good intentions unless they immediately degenerate into hard work." It's time to do the hard work of saving business from itself.

## LEARNING FROM GOOGLE

**If you** want your tools, processes, and structures to be more user centered, learn from the best. Here are Google's ten principles for a great user experience. (The principles are Google's; the descriptions that follow each are ours.)

1. *Focus on people—their lives, their work, their dreams.* Meaning that all your corporate tools must also help individuals achieve their own dreams and goals, not just corporate's goals for them.

2. *Every millisecond counts.* Workers must see that the use of corporate tools will save *them* time, not just save time for the company.

3. *Simplicity is powerful.* Simplicity as defined by the worker, not just by corporate.

4. *Engage beginners and attract experts.* The best experience in using corporate-designed tools and structures should appear quite simple on the surface but include powerful features for power users. Watch kids play a new game. They start by mashing all the buttons and seeing what happens. It's fun and easy and lets them learn what they need to know, fast. Your tools should work the same way.

5. *Dare to innovate.* Meaning encourage forbidden innovation. Find ways to incorporate what are currently benevolent hacks, then turn the hack around—make the changes available to everyone (with clear attribution for who "fixed the problem," of course).

6. *Design for the world.* User centered is so only if it is as diverse as all your audiences. If a process or tool

doesn't work for a country, region, or audience, you must invest in what will work.

7. *Plan for today's and tomorrow's business.* From Google: "[Our] designers . . . ensure that [our] business considerations integrate seamlessly with the goals of users. . . . If a profitable design doesn't please users, it's time to go back to the drawing board." Got it? Planning for tomorrow's business cannot be just about corporate's needs. There is no tomorrow's business without also meeting your workforce's (users') needs.

8. *Delight the eye without distracting the mind.* Engaging and even entertaining is good, but enlightenment and usability are key. If your tools are not easy to use, it doesn't matter how engaged your workers are—they still can't do their best.

9. *Be worthy of people's trust.* If employees forgo benevolent hacks and use all corporate-supplied tools and processes, can they trust that their careers and interests will be as advanced as much as the corporate goals will be?

10. *Add a human touch.* Executives who don't build a sense of humor, joy, quirkiness, and personality into their tools and infrastructure should be drawn and quartered, boiled in oil, then tickled until they give in. *Real people* use those tools! Allow room for the joy of being human!

## WORK-AROUNDS FROM THE FIELD

**Wikis, Wikis Everywhere** from Robert Rapplean: "I'm an all-purpose project manager. Most of my job is keeping track of the adjustments our company makes in our software products. My hack is to run as much of my job as I can through the wiki I built for my own use, ignoring most company-supplied tools."

Why I Wiki and Why Others Do the Same: "Since this is *my* wiki, I can organize it any way I want. I don't have to spend time negotiating with others over how it should be structured, and its organization is always something that I personally understand. It's become the primary method of tracking my progress for various projects and greatly improves my personal productivity."

On Push-back: "At the end of the day, all bosses really care about are results—high-quality, fast solutions, on time, and at or below budget. That's what I do, aided by my wiki. As long as I'm producing the results they need, whatever push-back I get from my boss and company is inconsequential."

On Benefits: Report Generation and Distribution: "All reports are produced online and readily visible to anyone at any time. This reduces the amount of time I have to spend in meetings rehashing what I told the other guys in another meeting two hours ago. Plus, as a bonus, if anyone nitpicks my spelling, my grammar, or the accuracy of what I have to say, I tell them, 'Thank you for spotting that! Please feel free to fix it.'"

On Benefits: All That Miscellaneous Information: "Since this is my wiki, it allows me to easily index and reindex, categorize and recategorize, as things evolve and the importance or irrelevance of information reveals itself."

(Rapplean had so many how-tos in his FastHack that we've continued it on HackingWork.com. There you'll find more about how wikis work, why you should use one to bypass corporate systems, and tips on how to get started.)

# HACKING THE WORLD

Never doubt that a small group of thoughtful, committed people can change the world.
Indeed, it is the only thing that ever has.

—Margaret Mead, cultural anthropologist

## SHOW IT, SHARE IT, SPREAD IT

Just north of the Golden Gate Bridge in San Francisco lie the Marin
Headlands. This book traces its ancestral roots to a weekend there
in 1984. Captain Crunch was there (John Draper, nicknamed for
his discovery that a toy whistle from a box of cereal produced just
the right tone to grant him free access to the phone system). So was
Apple's co-founder, Steve Wozniak, and Steven Levy, author of *Hackers: Heroes of the Computer Revolution*, as well as Stewart Brand, former Merry Prankster and publisher of the *Whole Earth Catalog* series.
The occasion was the first Hackers Conference.

Levy put forward a computer hacker's ethic, a single set of shared
values. Among them: Access to anything that might teach you something about how the world works should be unlimited and total; all
information should be free; hackers should be judged by their hacks,

not bogus criteria such as degrees, age, race, or position; mistrust authority, promote decentralization.[1]

Brand and Wozniak agreed, then added a nuance that would become the cornerstone of all workplace hacks. Stewart Brand: "On the one hand, information wants to be expensive, because it's so invaluable. The right information in the right place changes your life. On the other hand, information wants to be free, because the cost of getting it out is getting lower and lower all the time. So you have these two forces fighting against each other." Steve Wozniak replied, "Information should be free, but your time should not."[2]

Information is the object of almost every benevolent hack because it has the power to change your life. The company wants you to follow certain rules about how information is used because the compiling of it, adhering to it, and alignment around it is expensive and invaluable. Contained in that information are the strategies, rules, and practices of the firm. And in one form or another, most hacks try to free information from corporate restrictions so you can access it, interpret it, share it, and use it the way you need to, not just the way you're told to. The conundrum of these two forces, raised more than a quarter century ago, continues to this day.

Pull further back and you can see the cause we're all hacking for. Corporate infrastructure and resources need to find the right balance between just enough controls to manage costs and just enough freedom and flexibility so you can do what you need to do in a way that brings out your best. You need to hack because the system is currently out of whack—way too much in favor of the controls side. You also need to hack because corporate infrastructures treat your precious and limited time as a commodity to be spent, focused, leveraged, and wasted however the company sees fit.

Hacking is about finding a better balance between company needs and your needs.

## CHANGING THE DEBATE

As this book took shape, we discovered that its key messages and lessons to be learned were different from what we thought they would be.

At first, we thought Gen Y were the ultimate hackers. Then we discovered, no, hacking is happening because so many are feeling screwed—and that feeling transcends all generational, industry and job title boundaries. Then we thought everyone would feel empowered if we just showed them how to hack their way out of stupid-work. Whoa! Fear and anger ran rampant: "How dare you tell others how to work around what I believe is important?" . . . "How can I dare hack anything when I'm worried about my job?"

Dealing with those reactions—the fear, anger, and new questions about how to be responsible employees—taught us what this book was really about.

Power . . . Control . . . Risk.

Globalization and dozens of other forces have robbed organizations of predictability, stability, and control. So they push lots more controls and changes down through the company. React, push, control. React again, push more onto everyone, tighten the controls. This cycle is now repeating itself on an almost daily basis and has been in place for the past few decades. Still, for all the changes, everything always ends up in the same place—on the back of the individual employee. She is working almost entirely to ensure some institution's predictability, stability, and control while having next to none for herself.

She pleads with her manager for help, but his job is the same: Ensure the institution's predictability, stability, and control while having almost none for himself. He pleads with the senior team, but their job and the feeling of loss of personal control are the same.

So hacks start exploding as employees take back some control. And as soon as that's discussed publicly, everybody freaks out.

The system is broken. Everybody knows it and is being affected. Yet nobody's supposed to do anything? And we're not supposed to talk about what is being done? What's wrong with this picture?

The entire covenant relating to work, and the relationship among all the participants, needs to be rebooted. We've been running the same work contract operating system, with updates, since the industrial age. It's as if we've all been staring at the blue screen of death (also known as the "too broken to fix" error screen) for several decades. Enough already!

And don't expect business leaders to come to our rescue. You know what their solution is? Even more controls! According to CEO search firm Crist|Kolder, an outcome of the 2008–2009 financial crisis was the deepening of a trend that had begun a few years prior—eliminating their second-in-command positions such as COOs and division presidents and giving greater control over day-to-day operations to CEOs and chairmen.[3] And Six Sigma expert Anand Sharma, CEO of TBM Consulting, reports a 50% increase in requests to use Six Sigma controls as a way to deliver super-fast cost reductions.[4] React, push, tighten controls . . . welcome to our everlasting future.

Unless we do something to break the cycle.

We hope that every reader uses this book to hack the crap out of stupid-work and becomes a lot more productive and effective. (Legally, benevolently, and appropriately, of course. *Never* in a way that will get anyone sued. Got it?!)

But hacks cannot be the ultimate goal. We also need to change the global debate.

Consider yourself armed with ideas and tools to counter the most lopsided corporate controls. That's enough power to sit you at the table as leadership's equal. That's good. Companies respect power. That trumps "Be nice to us" almost every time.

Now that you have to be viewed as an equal, with the power of work-arounds backing you, we're asking you to actively change the discussion. Insist that we all talk about the unspeakables, the three great taboos.

Power . . . Control . . . Risk.

Is work an investment where power, control, and risk are distributed equally among all players? Or will it be forever maintained as a work-for-hire relationship where employers set the rules and employees are expected to genuflect and do as we're told?

Outing the hacking of work—showing you how to use what economist Joseph Schumpeter called "creative destruction" to change things *within* your company—means that people on all sides of this issue will have to discuss the *real* issues. The issues behind every hack:

- ► How much control should individuals surrender for the sake of a job, a paycheck, or benefits?
- ► At what point do corporate controls destroy our ability to control our own destiny?
- ► What's the right balance between the needs of the enterprise to thrive and survive and the same needs of the people within it?
- ► Why do corporate entities get so many ways to mitigate market risks when most individuals inside them don't?
- ► Leaders use worker assets—time, attention, ideas, knowledge, passion, energy, and social networks—to make their company go. Instead of just pay and benefits, why aren't we focused on ROI: the return the *workforce* deserves on their invested assets? Why aren't we talking about the ownership of and use of those assets?

If enough benevolent hackers raise these issues, *backed by their work-arounds that deliver results*, the debate will change. Getting the great taboos out in the open refocuses everyone on finding a better balance, on rebooting the work contract.

## WITH GREAT POWER
## COMES GREAT RESPONSIBILITY

Uncle Ben's warning to Peter Parker also applies to all us hackers.

Going to work means making choices. In the past, those choices used to be mainly: what industry, what career, what job, what company, how much money, how much benefits? Now that nearly everybody can hack almost everything, the choices are much bigger, reaching way beyond you and your family.

Even within someone else's company, everyone now has the power to be an entrepreneur or to change entrenched systems or to grow a business . . . or to do the opposite. Because you can now work around almost anything the company puts in place, you have as much power to destroy as to save, as much power to impede as to grow.

New technologies make all this a lot easier and a lot more accessible to the masses. Each individual's power and ability to leverage it has greatly increased over the past decade and will continue to grow over the coming decades. But the real issue is more timeless than technological advances and more universal than the employee/employer relationship.

You need to choose. Where's your ethical line? What would you do to control your own destiny: Will you work around *any* system and *any* barrier that wasn't designed with you and your teammates' needs in mind? What would you *not* do: Where is your personal line between benevolent and truly bad hacks? What contrarian's actions are *always good*, no matter what the boss says? What contrarian's actions are *always wrong*, no matter how noble his intent?

While every choice is ultimately up to each individual, as a society, as a workforce, as leaders, we all must contribute to establishing a new ethos for working together. This, too, must be part of the changed debate.

In the same way that medical advances have created new ethical dilemmas (When and how does life begin and end? . . . Just because we can change those things, should we?), technological advances in our work tools are way ahead of business's currently espoused code of ethics.

Every employee now has the power to work around almost any work system. Yet current work covenants pretend that that power does not exist. All employees are faced with daily dilemmas in balancing what's right for their customers, their company, themselves, their family, and their teammates. Current work covenants *preach* ethical decision making and yet—through their structures, systems, and tools—they rig the game so the only "correct" choice is what's in the best interest of the company. That sets up all of us. When everybody has to live a life that's out of whack, or game the system, or go outside of it just to meet personal needs, bad stuff happens.

If the covenant respected all parties equally and was equally enforced, a lot of senior executives would be forced to go back to the drawing board a lot more often. . . . And a lot more benevolent hackers would be seen as heroes—helping all of us to pull the system back to a place where it meets a lot more of everyone's needs.

A new mutually shared, mutually enforced covenant must be created—matching the realities of the New World of Work.

## START WITH THE END IN MIND

Whether you're reading this book from the potential hacker's perspective or from the perspective of managing and leading potential hackers, everything comes down to just one measure of success:

### "HOW EASY IS IT FOR ME TO DO GREAT WORK?"
- ► Emphasis on "easy" and "great."
- ► For most everyone in today's cluttered, chaotic, overloaded world filled with too many conflicting priorities, it's simply too hard to do their best. Great work requires easier work.

- Not "easy" in the sense that people or companies should lower their standards or that we should strip away the adversity that forces us all to new heights . . . absolutely not! "Easy" in the sense that companies and their tools and processes must be as user centered as they are currently corporate centered. "Easy" in the sense of unleashing the potential within each of us. Business's infrastructure must finally and truly address the barriers that stop all of us from doing our best work.
- If your work isn't easy, you should be hacking: Everything can and must be improved.

**We recommend a major overhaul of business measurements:** The criteria above—easy/great—need to be one of the top five internal measures adopted by every company. If that had happened five or ten years ago, this book would not now be necessary . . . most hackers would be finding a lot fewer things to hack.

There are almost no entrepreneurs or senior executives who would be willing to get their work done according to all the stupid rules, lousy tools, and pain-in-the-ass procedures that exist in business today. The design of work sucks!

In a world where information wants to be free and access is ubiquitous, the ability to excel no longer means being able to toil effectively against constraints built into our daily grind. Instead, the design of work must do a lot more to unleash our innate creativity, insights, and nature to set higher standards for ourselves than others would impose upon us. The work of the future must do more to increase the potential in all of us, as workers and as human beings.

Tomorrow's designs must live up to the unlimited potential within every individual. Which means the new ultimate measure in any workplace needs to be: "How easy is it for me to do great work?"

## THE PLACE TO BEGIN

Throughout this book, we tried to list tips for getting started so you could begin hacking right away. There also needs to be something bigger and more universally accessible, something that can be continuously updated. That's why we're going to close by sending you to **www.HackingWork.com**, as well as to any forum that works best for you—online and in person. We need to leverage them all.

We're asking you to continue what was begun here. We've identified three core themes that will quickly change the debate and do the most to advance the hacking of work as a positive force. Everything at HackingWork.com will revolve around these themes, and we hope you'll use them as a jumping-off point for your discussions wherever they occur.

1. **Town Square with a POV.** Town squares have always been gathering places for people to share what's on their minds and what's going on in their lives. Most modern online forums serve the same function, with one key difference. The best have a passionate point of view—they don't just provide the space to chat, they *sponsor the debate*. They provoke, prod, and guide the discussions. Most of all, they do it for the good of everyone.

   At HackingWork.com, we'll encourage all views on everything we've written here: pro, con, from senior executive and worker bee, and everything and everybody in between. Our goal is to be a feeder for the ideas and people who are actively rebooting the work contract and who are using hacking as a way to push for ever greater changes.

   Keep in mind that this loud, messy conversation is for a higher goal. As we've observed those conversations elsewhere, we've found the best to be Magna Carta–ish with a twist. The Magna Carta (Great Charter of Freedoms) is arguably one of the most significant documents in history in establishing obligations and freedoms between those in power and the populace. A century and a half after William the Conqueror centralized and organized power in England, the monarchy had grown so powerful that the landowners revolted. In 1215, their Magna Carta laid the foundation for many future bills of rights, constitutions, and limitations and responsibilities for those in power.

The higher-purpose goal is to strive for a Magna Carta kind of dialogue about the future of work—knowing that the process will be messy, noisy, and without a lot of reverence. That's what diversity of opinion can do: The highest value is not in everyone agreeing, but in the spirited debate, passions, and need for change that will move us forward.

2. **Toolkit for Bad Boys and Girls.** HackingWork.com and other trusted forums are places for you to share what's broken at work, and if you've hacked fixes, what they were. Or, if you're not sure what to do next, to post challenges you're facing and ask the community to chime in with their suggested hacks. We'll be watching how people rally around key ideas, and we'll showcase them in a "Best Practice" section—a catalog of the hacks that you most need to know, along with updates on how practices change as technologies and circumstances evolve. We'll also tag each entry as a Safe Zone or Red Zone practice, so you know ahead of time the degree of risk involved in each hack.

Take Nate's hack as an example: "In theory, I'm not supposed to moonlight [freelance] with any of my employer's competitors. In reality, that's just not practical—it places unfair restrictions on me, as everyone moonlights with everyone within our close-knit work community.

So I configured an HR terminal to change the noncompete clause in employment contracts *only* when my name appeared in the right spot and *only* on the way to the printer. After my contracts were printed, the changes were backed out with an auto undo. So HR's electronic noncompete file was pristine and untouched, but the copy I signed always permitted me to moonlight."

Would you vote Nate off your island, or would you buy him a beer, slap him on the back, and ask him how he did that? HackingWork.com will pick up where this book leaves off. Your participation will co-create the ultimate toolkit for fellow bad boys and girls. Your voice will determine whether hacks get voted as best practices or shunned and labeled as safe or risky.

Whether you participate in discussing your hacker's toolkit on our site or in the hallway in between meetings, the point is to out what's been underground for too long—for you, for your peers, and for everyone else who works.

3. **New Lens for Examining Work and Workplaces.** The history of computer hacking has been documented by many. But the history of hacking work has no record because it hasn't been outed until now. We're looking at something totally new, and if we're all successful, how we view the world of work will change.

For example: We've said that no one company has a code of ethics that we'd be comfortable recommending as a template for how employees should and should not co-create their infrastructures. While some companies are heading in the right direction, even the best of the best will have to reexamine their practices.

Look at Google as one example. We've applauded Google for their "20% time" policy, where many of their employees are encouraged and allowed to use up to 20% of their time to pursue whatever interests them. This is part of the new contract's call to turn over more control to employees in a way that also benefits the organization. Not only has this generated lots of product innovations for the company, but it also gives employees more control over how to best pursue what truly matters to them. Yet it wasn't until mid-2009 that Google management realized, "Hey, we don't have a good way to nurture these ideas through to completion." They finally instituted formal innovation reviews that would "force management to focus" on promising ideas at an early stage, said CEO Eric Schmidt.[5]

Even great companies and great leaps toward the new contract still have a long way to go.

Then there are unfolding technological issues that are going to have an increasing impact on every one of us.

Some examples: We've discussed your digital footprint as something that could be either an amazing advance in how you get work done (chapter 10) or the biggest innovation in controlling you since the first parent invented guilt trips (chapter 8). Currently, no one knows which way that will go. Also, there's tons of malevolent Black Hat hacking that needs to be outed and understood. Currently, too little is known about how bad work-arounds are affecting us all, and too few leaders are prepared to recognize the difference between good and bad hacks.

Which way will all these emerging forces go? Only time will tell, but HackingWork.com will be archiving and tracking how your efforts changed the world of work as it all unfolds.

We hope you'll join us.

# FINALLY: OUR WISH FOR YOU

We are hackers on a mission: to save business from itself and you from business.

Within the hacking community, that makes us Gray Hatters: people who act without malicious intent but publicize vulnerabilities in order to get the owner of the system to change.

As we hit "send" on this book, we hope the world spins a little smoother, the air and water are a little cleaner, sex is a little better, relationships are a little more meaningful, and life is a little more fun—all because we outed vulnerabilities within the system of work.

That last bit was serious—kind of. We're shooting for big change. But that ambitious goal is unattainable without you. If this book is going to make a difference, what you do next matters. Your hacks will matter. How your company embraces hackers like you and learns from you will matter. How you participate in the new debate matters.

It's time for work to adapt to you rather than you forever adapting to it. Show it, share it, spread it. Start hacking and let us know what happened.

# Postscript

## REPORTS FROM EARLY CONVERSATIONS

Nine months before *Hacking Work* hit bookstores, *Harvard Business Review* saw an early draft and named this book one of the top ten breakthrough ideas for 2010.

That meant even more opportunities to talk to people about what's behind benevolent hacking, and more opportunities to listen and learn. Here is what we took away from those conversations.

### 1. There's lots more hacking going on than we uncovered!

Benevolent hacking is the duct tape of the work world. It's the universal solution to every poorly designed and corporate-centered procedure, tool, rule, and process. If hackers stopped hacking, almost all business would grind to a halt. And if all hackers came out of the closet and shared what they are up to . . . wow, what a force to be reckoned with.

### 2. Most senior execs: "Yeah, but . . ."

"Yeah, our infrastructure is totally corporate centered. Yeah, that sucks for the workforce. But we gotta have our controls. What you're proposing is anarchy." Guys, we're just reporting what is already happening right under your nose. It's up to you to choose whether you view benevolent hackers as rogue rule breakers who must be contained or as a major competitive advantage to be leveraged. You already know what we think your competitors are doing.

### 3. Some midmanagers: "Yeah, but . . ."

"Yeah, hacking work could free me from tons of stupid-work and give me control of my life. But I've got 2.2 kids, a mortgage, and expensive habits I don't want to kick. I can't take the risk." Understood. Working around stupid-work isn't for everyone, and it can be a scary idea to grapple with. If you're not ready to take the plunge, we encourage you to hold onto this book until you are—we're hopeful that someday it will help you realize your passions.

### 4. Always remember: It's about change, not technology.

To alpha geeks, *Hacking Work* is like their world on training wheels. We get that. We didn't emphasize specific technologies for two reasons. First, detailed assessments of technologies, along with their how-to's, are better served and spread virally, through online forums. But more important—technology is just a powerful enabler. *Hacking Work* is about personal choice: Now that you know you can save business and succeed and work smarter by breaking stupid rules, will you?

# Acknowledgments

## THANK YOU!

Two guys hacking the future, one day at a time. These are the people who kept us grounded in reality as we pursued that lofty goal.

**From Bill:** Thank you Desi, Taylor, Stephen, and Ian for keeping Bill laughing, somewhat sane, and very loved and grounded throughout this project. Couldn't have done this without you!

**From both Bill and Josh:** To the work-in-progress counselors and readers: Someone had to tell us when we were on the wrong track and when our babblings were incoherent. Among a cast of hundreds, these folks deserve special mention for performing that service: Rick Bradley, Julian Chapman, Johan D'Haeseleer, Chris Ernst, Susan Flowers, Joe Fratoni, Phyllis Frazer, Sylvain Gauthier, David Horth, Lindsay Hurst, Dave Jardin, Cecil Johnson, Kim Jones, Mark Koskiniemi, Scott Leavitt, Mark Leyba, Lorraine Mahoney, Bruce Morton, Jim Phelan, Anna Pringle, Emma Reynolds, Sharrann Simmons, Janice Swift, Andy Szpekman, Graham Westwood. Thanks folks!

**To our book teammates:** We owe Dave Moldawer, Will Wiesser, Amanda Pritzker, Emily Angell, Mollie Glick, and the entire Port-folio team a huge thank-you. Will and Dave are the sages at Portfolio who "got" our vision and kept us honest to it. Amanda made sure this book got the marketing buzz it deserved. And Emily's attention to detail kept all our eyes on the prize. Mollie started it all: She's our book agent and so much more. Mollie took our original proposal and reshaped it so it actually made sense. Our thanks to all of you!

**To our book interviewees and anonymous contributors:** We didn't really author this book; you did. *Hacking Work* is your story. Thank you for sharing it with us so we could share it with the world. (And we'll keep our promise to keep you anonymous if that's how you wish to stay!)

# Notes

## CHAPTER 1: SAVING BUSINESS FROM ITSELF, ONE BAD ACT AT A TIME
1. IDC/*Fortune*, January 18, 2010.

## CHAPTER 3: WHAT'S NEW, WHAT'S NOT, WHAT'S THE MOST COMMON HACK?
1. *Home and Garden*, July 2009.
2. *Wall Street Journal*, November 16, 2009.

## CHAPTER 7: WHAT'S BROKEN NOW
1. *Time*, September 21, 2009.

## CHAPTER 8: WHAT'S AHEAD
1. One of the structural devices within this chapter—the questions "What's changing?" "What will be different because of the change?" "Who gains, who loses?"—comes from William Bridges, an expert on personal and organizational transitions. He argues that these three questions focus our hearts and minds on the most critical issues during times of transition.
2. MTV *Research and Strategic Insights 2009* report on Gen Y happiness.
3. Sources: Eurostat, *The Economist, BusinessWeek*.
4. *BusinessWeek*, December 15, 2008.
5. *Journal of Interactive Marketing*, summer 2004.
6. *Wall Street Journal*, October 2, 2009.
7. IBM 2009 global chief information officer study *The New Voice of the CIO*.
8. *BusinessWeek*, September 21, 2009.
9. http://smartblogs.com, "BlogWell preview: Nokia's Molly Schonthal."
10. www.ted.com.
11. www.cluetrain.com.

## CHAPTER 10: DEAR BOSS . . .
1. *BusinessWeek*, October 9, 2008.
2. Since most GE participants were not approved for participation, it would be difficult to statistically validate that their views were a representative sampling of the GE workforce. So this one company's findings can be discussed only for its illustrative

purposes. For a breakdown analysis of the questions asked and the study's findings, email the authors.

3. *BusinessWeek*, October 9, 2008.

4. *BusinessWeek*, July 13 and 20, 2009.

5. The New Work Contract from research for *Work 2.0* by Bill Jensen.

6. *Wall Street Journal*, February 28, 2008.

7. OECD, 2009.

8. OECD, World Bank, National Center for Education Statistics, 2008.

9. HR consultancy, Right Management, 2008.

10. *Foreign Policy* magazine, May/June 2009.

11. Multiple sources, most recent: *Manage Smarter* magazine and www.tdu.org

12. See www.Management-Issues.com.

13. *BusinessWeek*, June 1, 2009.

14. *Wall Street Journal*, January 26, 2009.

15. Jensen Group, *Search for a Simpler Way* ongoing study.

16. Ibid.

17. Ibid.

18. Ibid.

19. Basex.

20. See www.KeyCollege.com.

21. *BusinessWeek*, June 2, 2008.

## CHAPTER 11: STOP THE MADNESS NOW

1. See www.LeadershipIQ.com.

2. See www.PopTech.com.

## CHAPTER 12: HACKING THE WORLD

1. Fred Turner, Stanford University.

2. *Fortune* magazine, July 20, 2009.

3. *Wall Street Journal*, September 21, 2009.

4. *BusinessWeek*, September 21, 2009.

5. *Wall Street Journal*, June 18, 2009.

# Index